Re-Visioning Arts and Cultural Policy

Current Impasses and Future Directions

Re-Visioning Arts and Cultural Policy

Current Impasses and Future Directions

Jennifer Craik

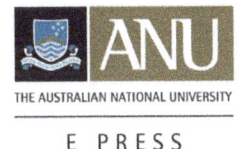

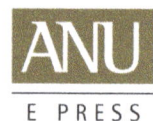 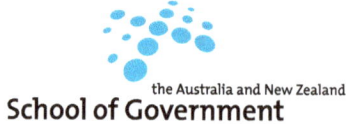

Published by ANU E Press
The Australian National University
Canberra ACT 0200, Australia
Email: anuepress@anu.edu.au
This title is also available online at: http://epress.anu.edu.au/revisioning_citation.html

National Library of Australia
Cataloguing-in-Publication entry

> Craik, Jennifer.
> Re-visioning arts and cultural policy : current impasses
> And future directions.
>
> Bibliography.
> ISBN 9781921313400 (pbk.).
> ISBN 9781921313394 (web).
>
> 1. Arts - Australia - Management. 2. Art patronage -
> Australia. 3. Government aid to the arts. 4. Art and
> state - Australia. 5. Australia - Cultural policy. I.
> Title.
>
> 306.47

All rights reserved. No part of this publication may be reproduced, stored in a retrieval system or transmitted in any form or by any means, electronic, mechanical, photocopying or otherwise, without the prior permission of the publisher.

Cover design, John Butcher
Sculpture: Aristide Maillol, La Montagne (The Mountain) 1937 (from a photo by Jennifer Craik)

Funding for this monograph series has been provided by the Australia and New Zealand School of Government Research Program.

This edition © 2007 ANU E Press

John Wanna, *Series Editor*

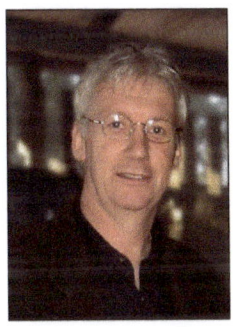

Professor John Wanna is the Sir John Bunting Chair of Public Administration at the Research School of Social Sciences at The Australian National University. He is the director of research for the Australian and New Zealand School of Government (ANZSOG). He is also a joint appointment with the Department of Politics and Public Policy at Griffith University and a principal researcher with two research centres: the Governance and Public Policy Research Centre and the nationally-funded Key Centre in Ethics, Law, Justice and Governance at Griffith University. Professor Wanna has produced around 17 books including two national text books on policy and public management. He has produced a number of research-based studies on budgeting and financial management including: *Budgetary Management and Control* (1990); *Managing Public Expenditure* (2000), *From Accounting to Accountability* (2001) and, most recently, *Controlling Public Expenditure* (2003). He has just completed a study of state level leadership covering all the state and territory leaders — entitled *Yes Premier: Labor leadership in Australia's states and territories* — and has edited a book on Westminster Legacies in Asia and the Pacific — *Westminster Legacies: Democracy and responsible government in Asia and the Pacific*. He was a chief investigator in a major Australian Research Council funded study of the Future of Governance in Australia (1999-2001) involving Griffith and the ANU. His research interests include Australian and comparative politics, public expenditure and budgeting, and government-business relations. He also writes on Australian politics in newspapers such as *The Australian*, *Courier-Mail* and *The Canberra Times* and has been a regular state political commentator on ABC radio and TV.

Table of Contents

About the Author	ix
Acknowledgements	xi
Foreword	xiii
Abbreviations and Acronyms	xvii
Chapter 1. The Conceptual ambivalence of art and culture	1
Chapter 2. Historical phases in arts and cultural policy-making in Australia	7
Chapter 3. The convergence of arts and cultural policy	25
Chapter 4. International trends in arts and cultural production and consumption	31
Chapter 5. How can cultural sub-sectors respond? Three indicative case studies	37
Chapter 6. Managing creativity and cultivating culture	49
Bibliography	59
Appendix A. Typology of artforms by characteristics of sector	73
Appendix B. Key moments in Australian arts and cultural policy development	75
Appendix C. Models of cultural policy	81
Appendix D. Definitions of cultural policy	83
Appendix E. The objectives of cultural policy	85
Appendix F. Government expenditure (Commonwealth, state and local) on the arts in Australia ($ million)	87
Appendix G. Summary of major inquiries into and reviews of Australian arts and cultural sectors	89

About the Author

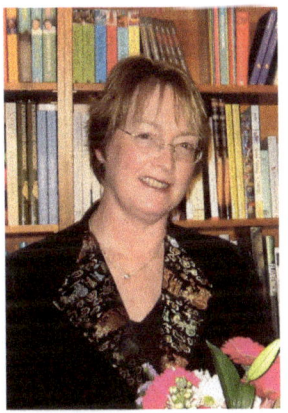

Jennifer Craik is Professor of Communication and Cultural Studies, School of Creative Communication at the University of Canberra and Adjunct Professor of Fashion and Textiles at the Royal Melbourne Institute of Technology. Her email: Jennifer.Craik@canberra.edu.au.

Professor Craik is a member of the Scientific Committee for International Cultural Policy Research which organises a biennial conference on cultural policy. She also is a member of *ConnectCP*, an online listing of international cultural policy experts. As a researcher, she investigates a number of areas of cultural studies and cultural policy, including arts and cultural policy, tourism, media, and fashion and dress. Her publications include *Uniforms Exposed: From Conformity to Transgression* (Berg, Oxford and New York, 2005), *The Face of Fashion: Cultural Studies in Fashion* (Routledge, London and New York, 1994); *Resorting to Tourism: Cultural Policies for Tourist Development in Australia* (Allen & Unwin, Sydney, 1991); *Public Voices, Private Interests: Australia's Media Policy* (co-edited with J. J. Bailey and A. Moran) (Allen & Unwin, Sydney, 1994); and *Cultural Policy Case Studies* (ed.) (Australian Key Centre for Cultural and Media Policy Studies, Griffith University, Brisbane 1997).

She edited the journal, *Culture and Policy*, between 1990 and 1996 and is a member of the editorial/advisory boards of a number of international journals: *Journal of Sustainable Tourism*; *Journal of Culture and Communication*; *Southern Review*; *Space and Culture*; *Tourist Studies*; *Museums Online*; *Leisure Studies*; and *Journal of Tourism and Cultural Change*.

Currently, Jennifer Craik is completing a book on *Fashion: The Key Concepts* for Berg Publishers.

Acknowledgements

Thanks are due to John Wanna for judicious editing and assistance with this monograph and to Evert Lindquist for generously giving his time to read a penultimate draft. I would also like to express my appreciation to the reviewers of earlier drafts whose comments and suggestions greatly assisted the production of this monograph.

I am also grateful for material, discussions and support from Clive Gray, Scott Prasser, Steven Boyle, Tim Rowse, Geir Vestheim, Christine Burton, Katia Segers, Katja Lindqvist, Paula Hunjet, Katya Johanson, Hilary Glow, Glenn Withers, Sharon Peoples and Jordan Williams. Some of the ideas underpinning this monograph were developed while teaching the Masters of Cultural Policy and the subject *Cultural Institutions, Industries and Policies* at Griffith University with Emma Felton, Robin Trotter, Peter Wynn Moylan and Terry Flew, whose contributions are acknowledged here.

The international perspective has been shaped by the International Scientific Committee for Cultural Policy Research, in particular, Oliver Bennett, Michael Volkerling, Per Mangset and Peter Dueland. Analysis of state contributions to Australian cultural policy has been stimulated by Jenny Menzies and Chris Bowen from Arts Queensland. I am also grateful to Claudia Scott and the ANZSOG masters students in *Designing Public Policies and Programs* (intakes 2004, 2005, 2006) for the opportunity to air many of the themes in this monograph.

I have been grateful for the infrastructural and collegial support of the School of Creative Communication at the University of Canberra. Thanks, too, for the comments of anonymous reviewers.

Foreword

In 2006, the internationally renowned cultural economist, David Throsby, published a paper called, 'Does Australia Need a Cultural Policy?' Its reception might have been relegated to minor coverage in the arts section of the print media except for the fact that it was launched by actress, Cate Blanchett. The occasion was initially covered enthusiastically until it was made clear that the Howard government was not amused by this cultural intervention. Sensing governmental unease, perhaps, an editorial in *The Australian* newspaper turned on the arts community with some vengeance, accusing it of not appreciating the Howard government's initiatives in cultural policy. Titled 'The Fine Art of Outrage: The Arts Industry are Unhappy – So it's Business as Usual', the editorial raged:

> There are times when arts industry insiders should take a bow for their contempt for everybody who does not agree with them. [They believe that] our lack of [government] support for artistic and cultural values has established us as a 'cultural pariah' ... It is easy to ignore arguments like these as mere masks, disguising demands for more funding. But they are also based in an assumption that *anybody who argues against the opinions of arts industry leaders on political issues is a philistine, or opposed to any critical questioning of our national identity*, generally both ... And saying some artforms are underfunded, according to their own estimates, does not mean we are irretrievably lost in a cultural desert. (Editorial, *The Australian*, 10 February, 2006, p. 17; my italics.)

Once again, the arts were on the front page and the subject of strong polarised opinions as to their intrinsic and national value. A recurring lament in public discourse in Australia (via talkback radio, letters to the editor or pub talk) is the claim that government expenditure on art and culture is a profound waste of money. Yet, such declarations prompt virulent defences of the *status quo* of arts funding, namely, that the arts and culture are public goods that create cultural vitality and national identity and, therefore, deserve adequate government support. This polarisation of opinions is the starting point of this monograph. It also has framed debates within government about whether to support and, if so, what kinds of support should be given to, the arts and cultural sector.

The consequence of this polarisation has been a tendency to treat the arts and cultural sector as a special case when it comes to analysing the profile of government support over time and between jurisdictions. In fact, the majority of analysts in this area have an *a priori* belief in the intrinsic value of the sector. Those who challenge existing support arrangements are dismissed as economic rationalists, philistines and hostile cynics. But is this justified? Why isn't the critical evaluation of current policy approaches seen as a valuable exercise? Why are disinterested analysts assumed to be against the sector? This monograph attempts to go some way towards persuading the sector, and its various analysts, to engage in a less partisan and more robust investigation of contemporary policies and likely policy prospects for arts and culture.

In short, the aim of this publication is to apply policy analytic approaches to the area of arts and culture. While some areas of public policy are well served by relevant policy literature, the arts and culture area has generally not received much attention from public policy analysts. The reasons for this may have to do with the intrinsic 'merit good' nature of arts and culture, or its relative lateness in developing as a policy sector, or even the marginality of arts to mainstream government agendas (O'Faircheallaigh, Wanna and Weller 1999: 273-289; Gray 2004). Whatever the reason, the sector is virtually neglected in public policy literature while most cultural policy literature (including cultural economics) is loosely disguised special pleading.

This monograph examines options for governments to respond to public debate about involvement in enhancing, fostering and shaping the artistic and cultural production and consumption of their jurisdictions. It explores the emerging bifurcation in national cultural policy directions. This bifurcation is characterised, on the one hand, by a regression to forms of old-style government patronage in supporting arts and cultural production, and, on the other, by the trend towards pushing arts and cultural practitioners to the marketplace with public taste becoming the *raison d'être* of creative practice. Policy discourses say to the sector: be excellent, be subsidised and be budget-dependent and/or be marketable, commercial and self-funding. But is this schizophrenic approach to arts and cultural policy sustainable? Are there viable alternatives? And, what are the long-term implications for policy-making in this sector?

The arts and cultural sector constantly battles a real dilemma in terms of policy attention. Arts and culture are often relatively minor concerns to government, yet they receive an inordinate amount of attention in the media and are frequently the focus of heated public debate (e.g. Carey 2005). Many governments from the late 1970s onwards adopted rational economic mantras derived from a stable of economic ideas variously called economic liberalism, neo-liberalism or, somewhat pejoratively, 'economic rationalism'. In essence, economic rationalism holds that the 'market' is a more effective mechanism to deliver choice and satisfy consumer preferences. While the market did not guarantee the absence of market failure, it was argued that it performed better than policy 'meddling' by politicians, bureaucrats or controllers.

The spectre of 'economic rationalism' has haunted the discussion of numerous public policy arenas, including the arts and cultural sector. In reality, the creation of market-oriented policies has resulted in a range of strategies designed to, inter alia, set limits to private legal and institutional activities, support competition, facilitate initiative, provide efficient infrastructure and provide a social safety net. At the very least, as Blandy noted, government retains a small role in the management of a society:

> This sort of involvement by government is different to what the anti-rational critics have in mind. In particular, laws and processes should be of *general applicability and benefit* and *not tailor-made* to suit the *special pleading* of various vested interests. If there is a case for a law to be changed, it should be a general case with a general applicability. (Richard Blandy, cited by Whitwell nd; my italics).

In other words, the theoretical objectives of economic rationalism have not been to throw governance to the wolves of the marketplace but to make laws that are general, not specific, and to use market mechanisms to change behaviour (e.g. via vouchers, tax incentives, commercialisation and/or partnerships).

In practice, however, governments have retained previous patterns of support while, at the same time, introducing new performance regimes and accountability measures. Although these have worked more or less effectively in some portfolio arenas, the arts and cultural sector has generally resented and resisted such perceived intrusions. Such 'patronage-with-strings' policies have been denounced vocally as examples of 'neo-liberalism', when in fact they are no such thing. Although government may wish to redefine or reduce its policy role with respect to the arts, a growing recognition of the contribution made by arts and culture to civic culture and national well-being drives increasing levels of policy engagement in this area.

So, although it can be argued that government policy since the 1970s has been suffused with the mantra/ideology of economic rationalism, the term has been erroneously applied to a multitude of policies, only some of which have truly been instances of economic rationalism. But the rhetoric has been powerful in re-defining the changing role of governments and the associated idea of the 'new governance'.

Moreover, as the cultural sector has been increasingly re-defined as cultural or creative *industries*, the potential economic benefits of cultural participation and practice have become a lure for governments keen to encourage new industry sectors. As a result, most governments feel that they need to be seen to be supportive of and engaged with the culture industries. But how do they do this without creating long-term dependency and nurturing industries based on permanent subsidisation?

As political commentators become preoccupied with the outcome of the upcoming 2007 federal election, arts and culture has once again come into focus with the Commonwealth Arts Minister, George Brandis, and Opposition Arts Spokesman, Peter Garrett, trading familiar insults and accusations at a University of Sydney forum on the future of arts funding in Australia (ABC 18/04/07, http://www.abc.net.au/lateline/content/2007/s1900941.htm). The government confirmed its preference for supporting elite arts organisations by announcing a one-off grant of $1 million to the Bell Shakespeare Company to fund its national Shakespeare education program. In effect, Bell was joining the Major Organisational Fund (the elite group of performing arts companies that are generously funded by the Australia Council in perpetuity) by the backdoor. While the elite arts sector has been the beneficiary of *de facto* government largesse, critics still decry the lack of support for second tier companies, grass roots companies, new artforms and individual artists.

In this monograph I am not advocating 'economic rationalist' or 'neo-liberal' policies. Instead, I am interested in investigating options that combine forms of government support with market-oriented measures in more imaginative and productive ways irrespective of the broad governmental agenda. Such strategies will inevitably involve a 'mix-and-match' composite of objectives, mechanisms, outcomes and evaluation measures. To achieve this, it is essential that strategies reject the 'old school' arts and cultural hierarchy that give rhetorical support to popular culture but insistently focuses schemes for government support into traditional, elite and non-popular forms of culture. This 'arts club' seeks to reproduce earlier forms of patronage under the guise of new governance, relying on self-serving arguments reminiscent of old-style lobbying. Alternatively, non-elite culture is treated as part of a general platform of cultural sustainability (that I prefer to call 'eco-culture' or 'pan-culture') and addressed in 'whole-of-government' or 'joined-up' governmental approaches.

This monograph addresses these questions and offers possible solutions to these dilemmas by taking a constructively critical view with an eye to the longer-term sustainability of the sector. While situating the monograph in an international context, specific reference is made to arts and culture in Australia, examining the role of government policy, specialist agencies, interest groups and cultural practitioners. I welcome the debate that should ensue.

Jennifer Craik
July 2007

Abbreviations and Acronyms

AbaF	Australian Business Arts Foundation
10BA	Tax incentive scheme for film production
ABC	Australian Broadcasting Corporation (formerly Commission)
ABS	Australian Bureau of Statistics
AFC	Australian Film Commission
AFI	Australian Film Institute
AGPS	Australian Government Printing Service
ANZSOG	Australian and New Zealand School of Government
ATSI	Aboriginal or Torres Strait Islander
ATSIC	Aboriginal and Torres Strait Islander Commission
CMC	Cultural Ministers Council
CMCSWG	Cultural Ministers Council Statistical Working Group
DCA	Department of Communications and the Arts (Australian Commonwealth)
DCITA	Department of Communications, Information Technology and the Arts (Australian Commonwealth)
DCMS	Department of Culture, Media and Sport (UK)
FCC	Australian Film Finance Corporation
FLIC	Film Licensed Investment Companies
IAC	Industries Assistance Commission (now Productivity Commission)
ICCPR	International Conference on Cultural Policy Research
MPAB	Major Performing Arts Board
MPAI	Major Performing Arts Inquiry
NCCRS	National Centre for Culture and Recreation Statistics
NGA	National Gallery of Australia
NMA	National Museum of Australia
OECD	Organisation for Economic Cooperation and Development
OzCo	Australia Council for the Arts
QAG	Queensland Art Gallery
SBS	Special Broadcasting Service
SMPA	Small to Medium Performing Arts

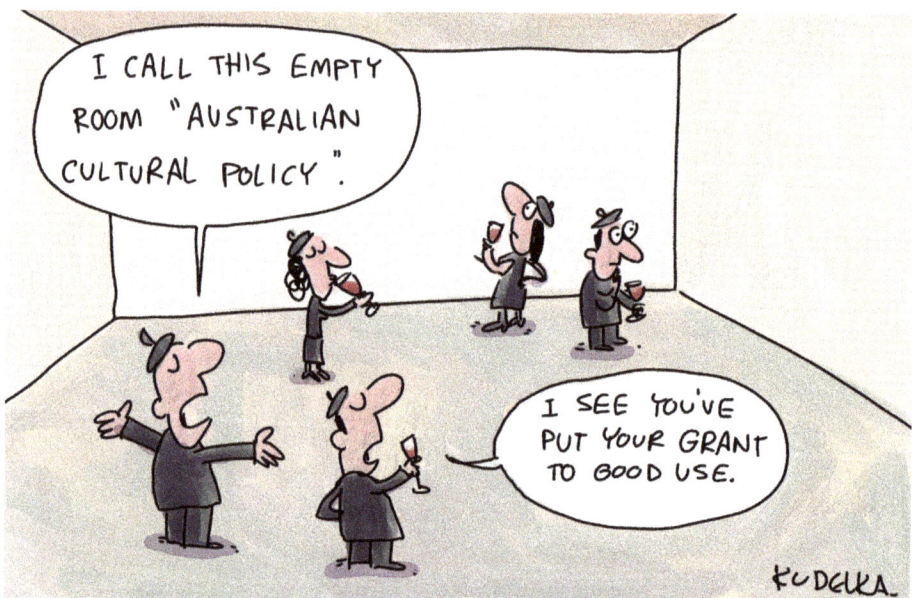

By John Kudelka. First published in 'Rear View' (*The Weekend Australian*) on 11-12 February 2006. Reproduced by permission of the artist.

Chapter 1: The Conceptual ambivalence of art and culture

Governments have traditionally worked with a 'limited palette' when framing options or designing programs aimed at supporting arts and culture. Historically and internationally, four models of cultural policy have predominated irrespective of either the cast or predisposition of government. These are: the *patron model*; the *architect model*; the *engineer model*; and the *facilitator model* (see Appendix C).[1]

States can act as *patron*, offering direct support to artistic and cultural forms favoured by the regime and tastemakers. This has the effect of nurturing and endorsing forms of art and culture deemed to epitomise *cultural excellence*. A variant of the patron model involves distributing funds indirectly, largely through 'arm's length' mechanisms such as through a niche, or specialist, arts council that relies on peer evaluations of cultural practitioners' excellence or worthiness. The UK, Canada, Australia and New Zealand as well as the Nordic countries have favoured this model for their national cultural policy mix.

For governments that choose to be more directive in shaping the development of culture, an *architect* model might be employed where culture becomes the responsibility of a dedicated ministry. This is a more interventionist approach in which the rhetoric and aims of arts and cultural policy might be broadly aligned with social welfare and national culture objectives. This enables direct government funding of culture and relieves creators from dependence on 'box office' mechanisms to survive. France and many other Western European countries epitomised this approach until the 1990s.

The *engineer* model is a more extreme, and politicised, form of cultural funding in which culture is prioritised as an objective of political education and allied with the ideological cast of the regime. In this case, government owns the artistic means of production and creators are employees whose creations are required to reflect positively on the political agenda of the state. Inevitably, culture produced under this model is overtly political and consistent with national priorities. Examples of the engineer model of cultural support include the former Soviet Union and other Eastern Bloc countries, Cuba, North and South Korea and China under Mao.

Alternatively, using a *facilitator model*, governments can opt for a 'hands off' approach in which the aim is to create the conditions that favour cultural production. In this model, cultural diversity is encouraged by indirectly supporting cultural patronage by a range of individuals and organisations, effectively subsidising cultural activities so they can survive commercially. A facilitation approach augments philanthropic approaches, largely by appropriating tax expenditures to provide tax relief or other benefits for those who give cultural support.

Although this model encourages diversity, it does not always ensure excellence since cultural philanthropy is often shaped by idiosyncratic tastes and judgments. The facilitator model can provide generous funding to cultural producers and operate more in tune with public taste and box office appeal, yet it is a model over which government has little control. The USA epitomised the facilitator model throughout the twentieth century.

In addition to the four models described above, we should add the *elite nurturer* model (Craik 1996). In this model, governments select a small number of elite cultural organisations to receive a one-line budget and/or other generous subsidies, thus placing them in a coveted position by guaranteeing recurrent funding that insulates them from having to compete with 'outsider' cultural organisations. On the other hand, as the nurtured organisations swallow up the majority of the cultural budget, there is little opportunity to fund new or experimental cultural forms, thus risking conservatism, or stasis, of cultural development.

Each of these models has strengths and weaknesses. Moreover, a number of changes have occurred over the last 20 years or so as previous models proved ineffective and new modes of governance have re-written the appropriate role of government in supporting culture. To some degree, a 'mix-and-match' approach has seen governments select aspects from different models to apply to different sub-sectors of the cultural domain (e.g. the sector development planning proposal by Arts Queensland, 2006). So, while the Arts Council in the UK remains the major cultural funding agency using an arms length mechanism, public lotteries established under the Blair Labour government provide significant amounts of cultural funding for other projects using a facilitator model, and still other monies are made available through architect-style cultural planning and community revitalisation strategies (Gray 2004, 2006; Lee 2006).

The precise mixture of policy models tends to reflect two particular features. On the one hand, cultural policy is predicated on social and economic arguments, that is, culture is posited as having 'positive effects on the economy, on social integration, on health, on criminal statistics, etc.' (Vestheim 2006: 10) while, on the other hand, cultural benefits have to be measurable or audited 'with evidence-based hard facts like number of tickets sold, box-office income, number of performances produced, actions to increase administrative efficiency, etc.' (Vestheim 2006: 10; cf. Belfiore 2004). Hence, there is now an emerging convergence on mixed policy approaches in most developed industrialised countries. For example, many European countries are:

> ... singing the same song. Some voices are stronger than others but even the weaker voices are singing to the same tune and the lyrics of the song are almost identical from country to country. Participation and access to culture for everybody is a good thing – especially if the supervision of the accounts can register a break even or better: profit. (Vestheim 2006: 10)

There is evidence of a growing belief that cultural institutions need to be re-invented to maintain their roles of collection and conservation and at the same time appeal to new audiences (cf. Obuljen 2006). The new audience for culture often lacks much cultural capital (knowledge of or interest in the cultural form on display). To engage with such audiences, cultural organisations emphasise entertainment and engagement above serious or detailed presentation.

One cultural institution that is currently going through a major re-invention is Amsterdam's Rijksmuseum, which is in the process of integrating its displays and material as 'an experiment in capturing the imagination of information-overloaded people with a low boredom threshold, but it won't be oversimplification' (Ronald de Leeuw quoted by Cosic 2006: 16). According to de Leeuw, museums have a new relevance for people in a multicultural society, tourists with short attention spans and school children on compulsory outings:

> People do need what I call a holy place,' he explains. 'Reading about something may give you a warm feeling or whet your interest, but you also like to test what you have read, to feel its existence in a place.' Churches, he says, are losing that sense of common ground; the town hall has become a glorified post office. But the museum can fill the vacuum. (Cosic 2006: 16)

Not all share this view. When the new director of the Louvre museum in Paris, Henri Loyrette, instigated policies designed to commercialise and popularise the activities of the museum, he attracted widespread condemnation for 'prostituting France's cultural patrimony for cash' (Cosic 2006a, 2007). By contrast, the architecturally unique Guggenheim museum in Bilbao, Spain, with its innovative and outreach cultural programs has generally been regarded as a major success. So, we can see that significant differences of opinion about how to manage culture in the contemporary world have underpinned and fuelled recent debates.

To fulfil these diverse expectations and experiences, cultural policy has developed a patchwork quilt approach to deliver multiple outcomes. For example, in Australia an arm's length *patronage* strategy (through the Australia Council) exists alongside an increasingly important *architect* strategy (through the federal Department of Communications, Information, Technology and the Arts (DCITA)). Furthermore, the interplay between patronage and the architect strategies can be complex as evidenced by the patronage role played by the Major

Organisational Facilities Board (now the Major Performing Arts Board) within the Australia Council but mandated by DCITA. A different mix characterises cultural policy in New Zealand where a creative industries model of cultural support vies with architect and facilitator models to disperse funds (Volkerling 2000, 2001).

In North America, Canada has pursued multiple strategies: the arm's length Canada Council, departmental architect/facilitator cultural development and local/provincial government cultural planning. Where philanthropic models of cultural support once reigned supreme, namely in the USA, diverse forms of cultural support have emerged with local government picking up a growing share of responsibility for cultural funding (Schuster 2002; McCarthy, Ondaatje, Zakaras and Brooks 2004).

By contrast, in Europe, where the government's role as a generous patron has been long established, changing economic circumstances are forcing cultural organisations to seek alternate sources of funding via sponsorship and partnership arrangements to make up for a declining share of government funding.

In sum, as Vestheim (2006) has noted, the 'advanced' (developed industrialised) nations are experimenting with mix-and-match models with varying degrees of success and all are immersed in the quest for an appropriate model for new times. There are many reasons why alternative models and sources of cultural support have not met expectations:

- potential patrons are often wary of experimental and controversial cultural forms while being willing to support more traditional forms thus further entrenching the *status quo*;
- philanthropic donors are more likely to sponsor defined products or events (e.g. exhibitions, festivals, commemorative events) rather than corporate costs associated with the activity;
- corporate donations and sponsorship are related to economic cycles and drop-off in straitened times;
- the potential for artistic interference from patrons underpins the dynamics of corporate support;
- tax expenditures cannot easily be targeted; and
- tax expenditure arrangements for culture are less attractive than for sport, festivals and community projects.

New notions of good governance have challenged assumptions that these are necessarily the best options for directing public resources to the support of the arts and culture. It is, therefore, useful to ask what differentiates the arts and culture from other policy domains? Does this sector require specific and distinctive policy solutions?

Although arts advocates often claim that government support for arts and culture is declining, available data suggest the reverse. In fact, it seems that governments are finding new ways to inject money into the sector (see Appendix F). How do we account for this paradox? The following chapter explores the ways in which policy trends for the sector have been affected by a broader operational definition of the arts and culture. We also examine the interplay between policy formulation and the increased availability of statistics and qualitative research about cultural participation. The conjunction of these phenomena has helped to frame debates about the implications for government of observed trends in the production and consumption of arts and culture. Also explored are shifts in policy responsibility for arts and culture within and between different levels of government.

ENDNOTES

[1] Using a more extensive taxonomy, John Pick (1986, 1988) characterized seven European models: Glory Model, Placebo Model, Educational Model, Reward Model, Service Model, Compensatory Model and Commercial Model.

Chapter 2: Historical phases in arts and cultural policy-making in Australia

Competing Models of Australian Cultural Policy

Australia has often been depicted as a cultural desert that only recently emerged from a bleak landscape and embraced cultural and creative practice as an important aspect of nation building. David Throsby, writing an overview for the Australian Year Book's 2000 edition (2001), for example, characterises three periods of Australian cultural policy:

- *1900-1967* when explicit policy was virtually *non-existent*;
- *1968-1990* when there was a period of *rapid expansion* of arts and cultural organisations and initiatives; and
- *1990-2000* witnessing further *moderate expansion* of the sector combined with the articulation of a broad cultural policy framework.

According to Throsby, the third period also coincided with an increasing interest in and availability of cultural statistics and the monitoring of cultural trends in the light of policy shifts. Throsby's focus, however, is essentially confined to the last few decades.

By contrast, Radbourne (1993) characterises Australian arts/cultural policy as a five-stage evolutionary process:

1. pre-war concern about the lack of cultural provision;
2. 1945-55 community intolerance about the lack of national theatre;
3. establishment of an 'inspectorate', a specialist bureaucratic organisation (Australia Council 1968–);
4. dynamic reform of cultural administration (1975–); and
5. directive management of cultural policy (1990–).

This is similar to Rowse's (1985) identification of distinctive *support funding strategies* that roughly equate to historical time periods: Voluntary Entrepreneurship, Statutory Patronage, Decentralised Patronage, and Dualism (see also Radbourne and Fraser 1996; Batterbsy 1980; Macdonnell 1992; Withers 1982).

It is argued here that a more nuanced chronology of Australian cultural policy may be more informative and appropriate (see Appendix B.1 and B.2). This chronology would encompass the following developments:

- pre-1900 settler culture emphasising nostalgia and a new beginning;
- 1900-39 state cultural entrepreneurship;
- 1940-54 the era of national cultural organisations;

- 1955-67 organisational patronage (through specialist bodies funded by government);
- 1967-74 policies of growth and facilitation;
- 1975-90 access and equity and community cultural development;
- 1991-95 diversity, excellence, cultural policy and cultural industries; and
- 1996- the review cycle and a return to neo-patronage.

In some cases, it is quite clear that governments pursued contradictory and competing agendas, not only from phase to phase but within phases. Moreover, similar policies have been adopted irrespective of which party was in power or what broad economic and ideological framework they operated within. Although there is a widespread view that Labor governments have been more sympathetic to the arts and culture, the evidence contradicts that view and reveals a much more complex and dynamic policy climate. While, broadly speaking, these depictions of distinct historical phases may be true and indicate a mounting interest, it is arguable that, in fact, Australian governments had from the earliest days a keen interest in arts and culture because this domain was associated with the development of a cultivated people and a national culture. However, in these early days, arts and cultural initiatives were not framed in specific cultural policy terms. Rather, policy interventions were *ad hoc* and *episodic*. To some degree, this situation persists in much of arts and cultural policy-making (cf. Rowse 1985).

Colonial Cultural Policies

Historically, specific events and characteristics made the arts and cultural sector in Australia distinctive. As a small yet dispersed settler society, colonial Australia lacked an esteemed aristocracy and social hierarchy that set the terms of cultural engagement, despite the best efforts of the self-appointed arbiters of taste. The nature of Australian culture was contested. While some yearned for a re-located English culture, others — especially ex-convicts and free settlers — were intent on establishing a non-aristocratic sense of social manners and cultural mores. Indicatively, the first painting purchased by the Queensland Art Gallery in 1896, *Evicted,* by British artist Blandford Fletcher, is described as 'a good example of Victorian social realism' (Queensland Art Gallery 1982:13, 48). It depicted a downcast mother and child unable to pay the rent being cast out of their home watched by neighbours and an unsympathetic landlord. The choice of this painting suggests that, even then, social comment and criticism was considered an important component of the cultural landscape even by the fine art sector.

As early as 1818 the fledgling colony anointed its first poet laureate, Michael Massey Robinson, albeit 'somewhat mockingly' according to Radbourne (1996: 12). Massey Robinson was a convict whose legal training and literary skills resulted in an early pardon. Despite his criminal background, he became registrar of all legal documents in the colony, a position with considerable benefits and autonomy (Throsby 2001; Clarke 1967). Clearly, the colony was in need of all the administrative skills it could get. As well as possessing legal skills, Robinson had a literary bent that he expressed in odes and poems. These idiosyncratic reflections became the first published literary works in Australia. In 1819, he was rewarded for his services with the gift of two cows. He is, therefore, credited with being the 'first recipient of an arts grant' in Australia (Throsby 2001).

The tale is also revealing in the fact that this status was granted by the colony's Governor Macquarie and not the English monarch. Equally, it was rescinded by his successor, Governor Brisbane. While most of Robinson's poems commemorated royal birthdays and milestones, he also wrote politically inflammatory poems and ballads (for which he was sentenced to Norfolk Island at one point) as well as poems that captured popular sentiments 'of what it meant to be a convict, and ... the ardent community spirit which informed Macquarie's Sydney' (Clarke 1967). In short, Robinson arguably set the tone of colonial cultural taste and reflected its desire to assert independence from the English heritage that had established the penal colony and shaped its early civilian character.

While this monograph cannot cover the scope of emerging cultural policy before Federation, it is clear that, beyond the struggle to establish the 'nuts and bolts' of a viable settlement, a considerable amount of energy was spent establishing the connotations of a 'civilised' society through clothing habits, domestic décor, furnishings, uniforms, the acquisition and production of artworks, and so on (see Maynard 1995). There was a profound ambivalence to this quest for civility evidenced by a reverence for the culture of Europe on the one hand and a heartfelt desire to be freed from the shackles of cultural elitism on the other. Perhaps inevitably, this produced a sense of 'cultural cringe' — embarrassment about nascent national culture — a sentiment that persists in some quarters today.

Nonetheless, colonial governments *did* support culture, for example, by establishing state art galleries (the first in Victoria in 1861 followed by New South Wales in 1871, South Australia in 1880, Queensland in 1895, Tasmania in 1887 and Western Australia in 1901). These galleries were given modest annual funds to operate and commence their collections (£550 for the Queensland Art Gallery, £1000 for the Art Gallery of Western Australia and £4000 for the Art Gallery of NSW), bolstered by private benefactions. By the 1950s, annual government support had increased significantly — to £22,000 for the Art Galleries of South Australia and Tasmania respectively, £46,000 to the Art Gallery of NSW and £70,000 to the National Gallery of Victoria (Throsby 2001).

Post-Federation Cultural Policies

Since Federation, the federal government has been committed to cultural support, as part of its mission of creating a national culture across its disparate and sparsely populated continent, through communications networks, media (especially the Australian Broadcasting Commission — the ABC – established in 1932) and in its role as cultural entrepreneur of broadcasts and tours of orchestras, theatre, and performing artists and so on. This role was gradually assumed by commercial entrepreneurs such as J. C. Williamson but the entrepreneurial role of government – especially (but not only) through the ABC – has continued.

The Commonwealth Literary Fund was the first federal grants body (1908) followed by the Commonwealth Art Advisory Board in 1912. As mass media forms developed, the federal government conducted inquiries into radio, cinema and performing arts, concerned as much with potential *harms* as with opportunities (see Appendix B). These concerns came to the fore during the Second World War when the Commonwealth made cultural regulation a priority of wartime policy (banning such things as American popular music – condemned as 'jungle music'[1] – and instituting stringent content controls on the media).

A desire to encourage Australian cultural production was recognised in the establishment of the first Arts Council of Australia – NSW branch (1943), National Archives (1944), National Film Board (1945) and state symphony orchestras (from 1946). There was also a campaign to establish a national theatre and/or arts council as part of the vision for postwar reconstruction (Johanson and Rentschler 2002: 168-9) but the election of the conservative government of Robert Menzies in 1949 put paid to that. Culture smacked of 'socialism'.

Post World War II Developments

Although the 1950s and early 1960s are often described as a 'cultural Ice Age', a number of elite national cultural organisations were set up during this period, including the Australian Elizabethan Theatre Trust, National Institute of Dramatic Art, Elizabethan Opera Company, the Australian Ballet, Union Theatre Company, Old Tote Company and the federal division of the Australia Council for the Arts (1964). This latter body was to become the key cultural organisation as a statutory authority in 1968, supported by various federal and state cultural organisations, while the states generally preferred using departmental arrangements to manage culture. These cultural agencies were both the product of vigorous *interest representation* and the symbol of a new moment of national culture, elevated in some cases, by the royal imprimatur. Australia was coming of age culturally, but still could not, or would not, sever its umbilical ties with England.

The importance of politically well-connected and persistent cultural lobbyists became a feature of Australian cultural policy both at federal and state level, a feature detailed by Rowse (1985) and Macdonnell (1992). These lobbyists were assisted by the formation of bodies representing sub-sectors of arts and culture such as writers, visual artists, Aboriginal and Torres Straight Islander (ATSI) cultural producers and so on. So, the polarisation of pro- and anti-arts and cultural interest groups persisted and has flavoured subsequent debates about national culture, cultural education and training, cultural development, multiculturalism, indigenous culture and cultural export.

It was at this point that things heated up on the cultural front and an energetic period of growth was facilitated by the Coalition governments of Harold Holt, John Gorton and William McMahon, and capitalised on by the cultural invigoration of Gough Whitlam's Labor government (1972-75) (see Rowse 1985; Macdonnell 1992; Gardiner-Garden 1994). This period saw the combination of an expanded role for the Australia Council, the emergence of specialist artform bodies, inquiries into performing arts, new innovations in the visual arts, film, television, crafts, museums, and in music. This panoply of energetic innovations set the scene for the later focus on access and equity that dominated cultural discourse well into the nineties.

As noted above, the idea to establish an arts council had been proposed much earlier, based on the perceived success of arts councils in Britain, Canada and New Zealand. They were heralded as a way to avoid idiosyncratic forms of patronage and determine cultural support on the basis of peer evaluation and excellence. It was considered that an arts council would be well-positioned to foster the development of national culture based on 'artistic merit' and democratic extension by providing assistance to cultural organisations and practitioners (Johanson and Rentschler 2002). Accordingly, the Australia Council for the Arts was composed of artform boards that evaluated applications for funding on the basis of peer review.

The Golden Years?

The 1960s and 1970s became known as the golden years for arts and cultural development in Australia. Funding across all levels of government rose substantially (see Appendix F) and many new initiatives were supported. It is important to note, however, that numerous initiatives, inquiries, reports and research commissioned under one government were inherited by succeeding governments which then had to respond initiatives not of their making. Consequently, it can be misleading to credit a particular government with responsibility for particular milestones when, in fact, they were initiated by the preceding administration. One example is the establishment of the Australia Council, proposed by Holt but (due to his untimely death) given effect by Gorton. Another is the scene-setting Industries Assistance Commission inquiry into the performing arts, commissioned by Whitlam, hijacked by the hardliners in the Industries Assistance Commission (IAC), and presented to an unsympathetic Fraser (see Appendix G.2 and below).

The invigoration of Australian cultural policy also faced the challenge of reversing the exodus of creative talent to overseas cultural Meccas. By the 1970s, this tendency slowed (although overseas experience and influences remain alluring to up-and-coming artists). It was now possible to envisage an artistic career in Australia. It was also a period of major social debate and change and issues like women's rights, youth culture, multiculturalism, anti-war sentiments, anti-capitalism and anti-colonialism were reflected in the debates about culture during this period. Australia's cultural landscape was transformed. The Australia Council expanded its role through a combination of state patronage and elite nurturing. Funding strategies were set in place. The largest share of funding went to elite organisations while individual practitioners competed for small grants.

Of course, not everyone agreed with this *new* Australia. To many it challenged sacred cows and championed suspicious new credos. Economic conservatives in central government agencies – The Treasury in particular – were especially wary. They tended to regard any expenditure on culture as a waste of public money but were even more alarmed at expenditure on what they regarded as radical and *avant garde* artforms. Moreover, all this new culture was inflating the cultural budget. Why, they argued, should government foot the bill to support creative workers who lacked a 'real job' to produce cultural entertainment for a few? This grumble gained traction in the 1970s as debates about levels of public expenditure and value for money began to influence the climate of policy-making.

Winds of Change

Under the Coalition government of Malcolm Fraser economic conservatism gained ascendancy, heralding a period of public sector restraint and cutbacks in government expenditure. Accordingly, the Industries Assistance Commission (IAC) was asked to investigate government funding of the performing arts sector. The IAC applied an explicitly rational economic model that rejected arguments about 'public good' and 'special pleading', instead viewing the sector as an 'industry' in order to assess its economic potential.

Perhaps surprisingly, the IAC rejected assumptions of cultural 'excellence' espoused by elite arts bodies and adopted a broader anthropological definition of culture incorporating concepts of national and community benefit. In abandoning the 'flagship philosophy' of existing cultural policy and advocating policies that reflected community values and the ordinary culture of citizens, the report recommended three new principles of cultural policy: *innovation, dissemination and education*. This meant re-directing support away from elite cultural bodies and towards objectives that aligned with community expectations and interests. In some ways, these recommendations were thoroughly modern and in line with the cultural sustainability arguments of recent times. Yet, the report has been 'misrepresented and misunderstood, [and] vilified' (Macdonnell 1992: 142-3), dismissed as *anti-arts, anti-patronage* and cast as the incarnation of all that is wrong with what later became known, pejoratively, as 'economic rationalism'.

The 1976 report created enormous controversy for a policy arena that had only recently begun to benefit from government largesse (e.g. Rowse 1985; Parsons 1987). Although the report fitted the new governance agenda of smaller government and self-sufficiency, it created an outcry about the inappropriateness of such a model for the arts/cultural sector. While its recommendations were repudiated by Fraser himself and ostensibly ignored by his government, the report nonetheless set the terms for policy during the next decade.

In a sense, Australian cultural policy became infused with the rhetoric of economic rationalism by stealth through strategies aimed at demonstrating community benefit, measuring performance and evaluating outcomes of government support. The ghost of the IAC report lingered in subsequent cultural policy-making. The intended outcome of the report (to wind back funding of elite culture and facilitate community cultural development) was stymied while the unintended outcome (maintain elite cultural support, impose accountability and shift from program to project and incentive funding) underpinned arts and cultural policy into the late 1990s. Specific developments in cultural policy became a tussle between influential lobbyists and sectoral interests, on the one hand, and instrumental policy-makers and outspoken critics, on the other.

Of all post-federation governments, it was the Labor Government led by Bob Hawke that was, arguably, responsible for the greatest changes in Australia's cultural policy landscape. Initially welcomed as a 'pro-culture Prime Minister', Bob Hawke did not share previous prime ministers' enthusiasms for the opera and the ballet. Rather, his sensibilities leaned more towards sport and everyday culture. He also oversaw an administration which had already undergone major culture changes and was beginning what was to become a long flirtation with managerialism. Governments had to be seen to be responsible in their spending of public money and to demonstrate greater efficiencies in activities they supported.

In the area of culture, Hawke set up inquiries into arts employment, youth arts, cultural statistics, orchestras, government funding, folk life and the indigenous arts and culture industry. This occurred against a broader backdrop of administrative and policy reform across all areas of government activity, centred on measures such as the application of performance measurement, the introduction of market incentives and corporatisation. The effect was the infusion of *facilitation* and *architect* strategies into an arts and culture policy mix that already contained elements of *patronage* and *commercialisation*.

Casting a 'Creative Nation'

These policy modalities continued under Paul Keating's Labor government. Although the so-called 'Keating awards' – designed to support leading artists by generous grants or incomes – attracted most attention, in fact, the most significant policy initiative was the release of *Creative Nation: Commonwealth Cultural Policy* in 1994. *Creative Nation*, arguably, marked the first occasion of an Australian federal government enunciating a clearly articulated cultural policy. In particular, it elaborated Keating's vision of a culture-led economic future in a globalised society (cf. Craik, Davis and Sunderland 2000: 195-196):

> Culture creates wealth ... Culture employs ... Culture adds value, it makes an essential contribution to innovation, marketing and design. It is a badge of our industry. The level of our creativity substantially determines our ability to adapt to new economic imperatives. (DCA 1994: 7)

The significance of *Creative Nation* lay in its dual emphasis on the national imperative to foster cultural development and the economic potential of cultural activity. It was not confined to the usual exclusive domain of fine arts and culture. Specifically, culture was identified as a key building block of national culture and individual citizenship. *Creative Nation* adopted an expansive definition of culture that included film, television, radio, multimedia, cultural heritage, cultural industries, libraries, indigenous culture, regional cultural outreach and cultural tourism. Initiatives for cognate issues such as education and training, copyright, export incentive schemes, taxation incentives, sponsorship and other facilitation schemes were also addressed. *Creative Nation* also addressed the role of the *Australia Council*, Commonwealth patterns of cultural support, the role of national cultural organisations, the performance and potential of diverse cultural industries, export potential and proposed a raft of new cultural programs and projects.

As a policy document, *Creative Nation* reflected the preoccupations of its time. In contrast to the earlier rhetoric of access and equity, cultural policy was cast in terms of cultural capital at both an individual and industry level. Significant sums were thrown at multimedia 'hothouses', designed to kick-start new generation technologies as cultural industries. Other policies that were implemented included the *Visions of Australia* and *Touring Australia* programs for visual art and performing art respectively, copyright law reform, and a restructure of the Australia Council. In addition, the federal Department of Communications, Information Technology and the Arts (DCITA) gained more traction as a policy leader and facilitator. Nonetheless, *Creative Nation* retained its commitment to excellence, now redefined in terms of international standards and success. To this end, national flagship companies came under new funding and administrative arrangements, most significantly through the Australia

Council's *Major Organisations Fund*, the creation of which aggravated cultural interest groups and lobbyists. As a consequence, the Fund was criticised as a return to elitism and favouritism and an abandonment of more prosaic forms of culture.

This policy direction was part of the Labor government's philosophy of targeting under-performing or under-resourced areas by shoring up national cultural organisations as well as facilitating citizen engagement with culture. At the same time, the government was committed to reforming the sector in industry terms stressing the capacity to generate export growth in the global cultural marketplace. This strategy was underpinned by an increasingly sophisticated understanding of cultural practice and consumption, informed by commissioned research. This research also informed the critique and revision of government approaches to cultural support.

The Keating government lost office before it had implemented much of *Creative Nation*. By the end of the Keating government, the arts were rhetorically associated with Labor: cultural practitioners were believed to be of 'left' persuasion while Labor governments were perceived to endorse proactive arts and cultural policy. To some extent (as Appendix B shows) this assumption was a myth, yet it had important consequences for the direction of cultural policy after Keating.

An Alternative Vision for the Arts

Reacting to the 'Arts for Labor' mantra and reflecting their economic rationalist thinking, the Coalition in opposition endorsed a hardline arts policy in 1993 as part of the *Fightback!* portfolio of policies that advocated kneecapping the Australia Council and devolving arts funding to the states (see exhibit 1). This document enthusiastically embraced the tenets of economic rationalism. Cultural agencies were to be cut adrift from the steady drip of public money and forced to compete in the marketplace. Strong adverse reaction to this hardline policy at the 1993 election, especially from influential conservative cultural lobbyists, persuaded the Coalition to reconsider this policy approach and adopt a softer line.[2]

Exhibit 1: *Fightback!* The 1993 Coalition *Vision for the Arts in Australia*

In March 1993, the Coalition opposition released its Arts policy as part of its *Fightback Australia!* platform in the lead-up to the March election. At the time, John Hewson, a committed economic rationalist, was Liberal Party leader and Senator Michael Baume was opposition arts spokesman. *A Vision for the Arts in Australia* was a bold document designed to counteract Prime Minister Paul Keating's underwriting of an expert panel that was developing a Commonwealth statement of cultural policy (*Creative Nation* was published in 1994).

The pressure to re-think arts and cultural policy arose from successive debates in parliament, the media and within the arts community. This policy sought to: clarify the respective roles of Federal, state and local government; redress declining Federal funding to the Arts and Cultural Heritage area; quell controversy about grant funding to trade union organisations; address the perception of inadequate allocation of funds to community arts by the Australia Council; and counter general unrest about the direction of the Australia Council under Rodney Hall's chairmanship. A ghost that shadowed this debate was former opposition arts' minister Chris Puplick's declaration in 1988 that the Australia Council should be abolished. Although this policy was later retracted, the fallout from this statement framed the reaction to the subsequent Coalition arts policy.

The public and media impression of the *Visions* document was that the Coalition was committed to savaging support for art and culture by such measures as:

- shifting funding of national organisations to the Federal department;
- restructuring the Australia Council to redress peer review mechanisms, and provide incentive payments rather than grants;
- shifting the funding of non-national arts organisations to the states;
- underwriting national and international touring programs; and
- enhancing tax incentive schemes to encourage private investment and involvement in the arts.

The policy was also committed to supporting youth arts, folk heritage, popular music and pushing the film industry towards a private sector and commercial underpinning. Rather than repudiating the arts, this policy explicitly confirmed the Coalition's commitment to the arts, and acknowledged the importance of culture in national identity, the pursuit of excellence in the arts and centrality of art and culture in international perceptions of Australia. But it also observed that 'the great bulk of arts activity in Australia proceeds without the need for taxpayer support' (The Coalition Arts Policy 'An agenda for the arts' 1993). This was perhaps the greatest un-stated threat to the cosy arrangement enjoyed by the arts fraternity with arts funding organisations.

In fact, the *Vision* document advocated a major shift in mechanisms of support from the 'drip feed' model of grants and direct funding to matching funding, tax incentive and audience-oriented forms of support. The policy also advocated a range of accountability, duplication of services and market-sensitive schemes to evaluate the effectiveness of support mechanisms and eliminate the perceived rampant cronyism and cliquey behaviour of grant bodies such as the Australia Council. The document concluded by quoting John Hewson's promise not 'to inhibit the further growth of our arts and cultural industries' but to let 'the arts industry in Australia ... thrive and grow' (The Coalition Arts Policy 'Executive Summary' 1993: 11).

Reaction to the *Vision* document was heated and sustained. The arts community was supported by influential media, commentators who condemned the Coalition policy, in particular, its threat to the Australia Council and the statutory independence of the arts. Further controversy raged over the anticipated negative impact of a GST on the arts sector. United opposition to the Coalition policy was sealed by the Government's release of its election cultural policy, *Distinctly Australian, The Future of Australia's Cultural Development* which anticipated a commitment to a comprehensive cultural policy and re-evaluation of arts and culture as vibrant and economically valuable cultural industries. By the time of the election, the arts community had come out strongly in support of the Keating government and was believed to have influenced the election outcome and Labor's victory.

Despite the enthusiasm of the arts community for the government, the next budget delivered little to the sector with funding remaining virtually unchanged. Indeed, Senator Baume claimed that the only increase in funding was to the 'Keating' fellowships. Baume himself had distanced himself from the *Vision* document in the lead-up to the election on the basis of the negative press it attracted and had lobbied unsuccessfully for Hewson to revise the policy. After the election, Hewson took on the arts portfolio himself while Baume continued to profess unease with the Coalition's policy from the backbench and in his retirement.

In all, the significance of the *A Vision for the Arts in Australia* was profound, galvanising the arts community into an effective and relentless lobbying network wedded to increasingly outdated patronage models

> of arts funding and resisting attempts to devise new philosophies and mechanisms of support. The fact that the reaction of the arts community was based on a misunderstanding of the *Visions* document makes the controversial role it has in Australian cultural policy all the more ironic.

When elected in 1996, the incoming Howard government lacked a coherent cultural policy of its own, so much of the thrust of *Creative Nation* continued to drive cultural policy at the coalface, though not by that name. Cultural lobbyists and interest bodies resumed their courting of government. Cultural agencies continued, somewhat uncertainly, to manage on reduced budgets. Cultural practitioners continued to be trained and aspire to a cultural profession. Cultural export continued to be favoured by government although Howard was less interested in the new 'Asian Tigers' (so enthusiastically embraced by Keating) and was more at home in re-connecting with Europe and North America. Culture continued to be supported and the Howard government gradually evolved its own elite nurturer-cum-architect model that culminated in the decision to build a new national cultural institution in Canberra, the National Portrait Gallery (of which his wife was patron).

Meanwhile, *Creative Nation* lived on as an important policy learning tool not only for state and local governments in Australia but also internationally. The document shaped the incoming Blair Labour government's arts and cultural policy in Britain, for example. Its philosophy and strategies were copied by local think tanks that influenced the *facilitation* and *architect* models adopted by the UK's Department of Culture, Media and Sport (DCMS 2004). In contrast, there was a lack of arts and cultural policy direction in the Coalition government in Australia nationally (see Borghino 1999; Marr 2006; Strickland 2004) and the sector muddled along at the federal level while the states and local government became more proactive and innovative (Craik, Davis, Sunderland 2000). Ironically, the *intent* of the IAC report was at last being implemented.

Cultural Policy for the New Millennium

Over time, the Howard government shaped a new policy framework — virtually by default. Changing governance requirements, a lack of success in promoting cultural industries and the rising costs of maintaining and operating cultural facilities, the difficulty of reconciling commitments to social inclusion versus cultural diversity, all combined to prompt the government to take (belated) charge of cultural development.

The Howard government resorted to an aggressive gamble on elite cultural organisations and, concurrently, promoted a *policy 'attachment' approach* in which arts and cultural activities would form a part of policy delivery strategies targeting unemployment, health, environmental sustainability and training

(Gray 2004, 2006). Effort was also invested in producing cultural statistics (e.g. the Australia Council's *Australians and the Arts*, reports by the Cultural Ministers' Council, and reports on cultural participation by the Australian Bureau of Statistics). Although the Howard government's three-pronged approach to arts and culture amounted, to a large extent, to an 'unofficial' policy, it nevertheless carried significant implications for re-shaping the arts and cultural sector.

From 1998, the government initiated, in an ostensibly *ad hoc* way, what became *the review cycle* of major elite cultural forms (performing arts, visual arts and crafts, new media, orchestras, and so on) (Strickland 2004). This approach was engineered by then Minister for Communication, Information Economy and the Arts, Richard Alston, who realised that the major flagship cultural companies 'were teetering on the verge of financial collapse' and needed a 'business' analysis of their performance and potential. A formal inquiry into Australia's major performing arts conducted by Helen Nugent and published in 1999 (*Securing the Future*, also referred to as the *Nugent Report*) provided a rigorous 'warts and all' critique yet, surprisingly, resulted in 'a $70 million injection' into the sector by federal and state governments. According to Strickland (2004: 9):

> The Howard model for arts funding was set: if arts organisations wanted more money from government, they should forgo warm, fuzzy talk and instead build a business case based on thorough research.

Reviews were subsequently commissioned for the following sectors: visual arts and crafts, symphony orchestras, music education, opera, new media, the small-to-medium sector and dance (see Appendix G). Although the Howard government was perceived to be anti-arts, in fact:

> Through its review-driven cultural agenda the Howard government has given the arts greater funding than most governments. Its record for injecting extra funds into the arts is impressive, up there with the Whitlam, Keating, Kennett [Victoria] and Dunstan [South Australia] administrations. (Strickland 2004: 9)

The perception lingered that the Howard government was not favourably disposed towards the arts (Caust 2006; Glow and Johanson 2006) and that, unless a particular sector had secured a review and subsequent special treatment, there was little hope of government largesse for other sub-sectors. Overall, there was no vision for arts and culture – 'no inspiring blueprint for the role culture could play in fostering a dynamic society' (Strickland 2004: 9). Instead, the government placed its bets on the 'Big End' of town – national cultural organisations that were visible, elite-oriented and represented by effective lobbyists.

Elite nurturing was the outcome of the review cycle with a new emphasis on specialist financial shepherding of selected organisations under the Major Organisational Bodies fund of the Australia Council. In 2000, Australian Business

Arts Foundation (AbaF) replaced the Australia Foundation for Culture and Humanities in an attempt to encourage the private sector to support the arts and cultural sector by sponsorship and partnership arrangements. This was an attempt to develop alternate models to government support for the arts (facilitation and architect). While AbaF has received positive coverage, it is still dependent on government support as an agency. Indeed, its budget has grown annually in contrast to many other arts and cultural agencies. Most recipients of AbaF sponsorship awards have gone to the 'Big End' of the culture business and, arguably, exacerbated the plight of small and medium arts and cultural organisations. The new style of arts policy that has emerged from this period has been described as 'a cosy arts-business love match' (Perkin 2006: 19), a combination of elite nurturing, facilitation and architect, or what I have called elsewhere a 'neo-patronage' model of support (Craik 2006; cf. Perkin 2007a,c).

Cultural funding by government has increased throughout the century, especially since the Second World War. This has been the case even in the face of the managerialist and economic rationalist policy formulations of recent governments. However, because of the expanding definition of culture and the expanded role of culture, there is more competition for support and, thus, less is available for particular organisations. Moreover, funding has devolved from federal to state and local governments, especially in certain sub-sectors, such that patterns of support and funding are increasingly a reflection of regional and local priorities rather than national agendas (cf. Schuster 2002; National Centre for Culture and Recreation Statistics 2005; Arts Queensland 2006). The exception is the *Major Performing Arts* program where selected national cultural organisations are funded under special favourable conditions.

The Major Performing Arts Sector Spearhead Policy About-Face

A review of the Major Performing Arts (MPA) companies (Australia Council 2003) purportedly showed that the companies had improved their performance in terms of artistic vibrancy, access and financial viability. In fact, a detailed examination of the data suggests a mixed outcome with annual fluctuations in the number of new works, the proportion of Australian works, participation and measures of effective 'outreach'. Most worrying are the financial results, which show that there are fluctuations in box office income, private sector income and assets while 'aggregate negative net assets have increased by 74%' meaning increasing *deficit*s across the companies in just four years (Major Performing Arts Board 2004: 17). The cost of companies 'doing more' – as required by the 'tied' nature of funding (e.g. touring, commercialising, exporting, etc.) on top of escalating overheads (salaries, training, administration, infrastructure maintenance, etc.) has aggravated financial viability.

Thus, irrespective of performance and auditing requirements, the performance of these companies is continuing to falter at an alarming rate. Costs are outstripping income, repertoire is becoming more conservative and less Australian, and free tickets still artificially bolster attendance figures. Moreover, the reliance on subsidised seats noted in the *Nugent Report* — from $25 per seat in Sydney and Melbourne to $282 per seat in Hobart across all the performing arts (dance, music, opera and theatre) — remains essential to inflate the audience aggregate.

The most parlous situation is in the area of symphony orchestras, which were conveniently omitted in the MPA review but have been analysed elsewhere (Boyle 2006). Boyle concluded that productivity has barely increased, while audiences are continuing to decline (as well as aging and not being replaced by a younger cohort). Indeed, he concluded that 'the classical music attender has become increasingly marginalised' (Boyle 2006: 16). More worryingly, his analysis shows that organisational costs have doubled and, although revenue has tripled, organisations have only been kept afloat because of increasing (compensatory) government subsidy. In short:

> ... the various changes in organisational structure have not been effective in addressing the cultural objectives of increasing audience attendance or performance levels. However, they have been more effective in attaining economic objectives of diversifying the funding base and increasing earned revenue opportunities, but not in creating cost efficiencies. (Boyle 2006: 17)

We are, thus, left with a conflicted situation in which major performing arts companies are beneficiaries of a special arrangement for funding and support that is both ineffective and monopolises the limited resources of key cultural administrative organisations such as the Australia Council and DCITA. Meanwhile, instrumentalist *policy attachment* strategies sit uneasily alongside *elite nurturing* approaches, such as that embodied in the MPA funding strategy. Furthermore, cultural statistics provide evidence of the organic and dynamic nature of cultural participation, consumption and production that challenges the underlying philosophy of much arts and cultural policy.

A consequence of these developments is that management of the MPA funding protocols now forms an increased proportion of the activities of the Australia Council to the ultimate cost of other artforms and support functions. It has, as a result, become a more insular organisation: inward looking and resistant to external scrutiny or engagement. Moreover, the Australia Council resists innovation and is perceived to be out of touch with developments in newer and competing artforms (Gallasch 2005; Glow and Johanson 2006; Marr 2005). Perhaps the siege mentality exhibited by the Australia Council arises from it arm's length approach. More likely, it arises from the fact that the Council is in direct competition with DCITA for the role of leading cultural agency for, indeed, many of its roles and functions could easily be absorbed by the department. In short, the Australia Council may be — as an agency structure — out of synch with arts and cultural policy today and the needs of cultural development in the future (cf. Craik 2006).

A major restructure of the Australia Council in 2005 was designed to address some of its perceived failings (Australia Council 2005a, b). At the heart of the restructure was the decision to abolish two of its artform boards: Community Cultural Development and New Media Arts. Yet, this was an odd decision given that these two boards were:

> The newest and least conservative. Both these boards evolved to get around the failures of the old structure, which had become too anachronistic. (Marcus Westbury, artistic director of Melbourne's Next Wave Festival, quoted by Dimasi and Paech 2004)

Former Deputy Chair of the Australia Council, Lex Marinos, observed: 'They are effectively taking away the opportunity for local communities to partake in their cultural expression.' He also called the move 'retrogressive', and added, 'I'd like to think if a sensible debate can be had, there is a possibility to reverse the decision that is disadvantaging a lot of Australia' (Dimasi & Paech 2004).

The abolition of two innovative artform boards certainly seemed to contradict the stated intention of the restructure, namely to position:

> ... the Council as an 'arts catalyst', an agent of support and change for the arts in Australia, and a more flexible, well-informed and responsive organisation ... designed to engage more Australians in the arts, deliver the arts to more Australians, and help shape a more vital and sustainable arts sector. (Australia Council 2005b)

Despite the optimism of then CEO, Jennifer Bott, and then Chairman, David Gonski, there is little evidence that the restructure has achieved its aim of:

> Moving away from a rigid model of grants and services towards one with far greater flexibility and more about innovative ideas and partnerships. (Gonski quoted in Australia Council 2005a)

Rather, it might be argued that the 'new look' Australia Council is further alienated from its clients and the broader arts and cultural community of interest — not to mention from public opinion and media analysts. The restructure was more about *bureau politics* than policy reform. In short, the Australia Council's fortress mentality and isolation within the cultural sector suggest that it is a victim of the lack of direction in the policy arena. The appointment of Kathy Keele, former CEO of AbaF, as the CEO of the Australia Council, reflected a desire of the government to consolidate the 'neo-patronage' model and 'forge closer ties with the business community as a way of generating cash support for the low-income sector' (Perkin 2007b: 44. See also Keele, 2005).

Perhaps there is a need to create competition among cultural agencies to offer a range of support strategies for which cultural practitioners and organisations compete. This has occurred with the decision to fund a new building for the National Portrait Gallery in the parliamentary triangle of Canberra. This Gallery now challenges the pre-eminence of the National Gallery of Australia, the National Library of Australia and the National Museum of Australia as having the 'right' to stage definitive exhibitions of visual art that reflects national culture.[3]

From Incremental Creep to Interventionary Strategies

Arts and cultural policy under the Howard Coalition government can thus be characterised as a shift from 'incremental creep' to multi-pronged interventionist program involving four initiatives. The first was the 'review cycle' of sub-sectors in trouble; the second was the 'cosy arts-business love match' between businesses sponsoring or partnering with cultural organisations; the third was the return to 'neo-patronage' in the form of special assistance to selected major national cultural organisations under the Major Performing Arts program; and the fourth was the advocacy of 'eco-culture' or instrumental policy attachments between culture and adjacent sectors. This platform of policies has the potential to radically re-cast the arts and cultural sector and the terms of government engagement with the sector. Yet, so far, this new vision has not been spelled out and *ad hoc* 'back of the envelope' policy-making remains. So, despite all the changes in policy models, strategic planning, accountability and rhetoric, the arts and cultural sector still has no clear policy road to follow.

ENDNOTES

[1] There was a moral panic that 'black' American music would incite the passions of impressionable young (female) Australians particularly where American troops were stationed in Australian cities such as Brisbane.

[2] Pauline Hansen's One Nation party was also perceived as a threat and litmus test of popular opinion in Australia and she, too, proposed radically cutting arts and cultural funding.

[3] An example occurred in 2004 when there were exhibitions of leading Australian women artists held simultaneously but independently by the NGA (Grace Cossington Smith), NPG (Thea Proctor), NLA (Olive Cotton) and NMA (Margaret Preston). Another case of competition leading to dynamism occurred in Brisbane when the Museum of Brisbane was established in 2001. There was heated opposition from the Queensland Museum to the creation of this 'upstart' that quickly gained a reputation for innovative exhibitions, outreach programs and community engagement. This forced the QM to initiate a major overhaul of its program and permanent exhibitions (although this seems to have produced major changes in the building, its new exhibitions and activities are as staid as before).

Chapter 3: The convergence of arts and cultural policy

While the previous chapter focused on arts and cultural policy in Australia, there are parallels in many other countries. Governments of all persuasions, in all jurisdictions have experienced difficulty in formulating coherent and appropriate policy strategies for the arts and cultural sector. In particular, in most developed countries, support for the elite arts has been allied to a range of *instrumental* strategies in which cultural and creative activities are used to leverage solutions to a variety of social problems. These include unemployment, social alienation, regional access, disability, social welfare and therapy, and more generally, the creation of a sense of community and 'well-being'.

Re-Visioning 'Culture'

In the United Kingdom, according to former Minister for Culture, Tessa Jowell, there has been a major shift in the arguments and strategies for under-writing culture — from support for culture on the basis of 'what it does in itself' to support for culture 'in terms of its instrumental benefits to other agendas' (Jowell 2004: par.12-13). Jowell argues that the result of this policy shift has been 'a spiral of decline' (Jowell 2004: par.24). Whether culture is supported because of its 'intrinsic value' or its 'instrumental benefits', Jowell's successor, David Lammy, argues that 'we still lack a coherent case' to justify government investment in culture (Lammy 2006: par.19). So, on the one hand, government support is still assumed to be worthy and the sign of a 'civilised' regime while, on the other, support is decried as an indulgence of so-called 'bleeding hearts'.

Possible reasons why cultural and creative organisations have found it harder to be sustainable might include:

- they are spread too thinly doing too many things; or
- pressure from competition with other agencies pursuing instrumental programs; or
- the broad brush approach undermines the original cultural or creative rationale of particular organisations or cultural practitioners.

It is also the case that governments in many jurisdictions have attempted to reduce the reliance of the arts and cultural sector on the public purse by facilitation and incentive policies designed to increase support from the private and non-government sectors. At the same time, increases in the number of cultural organisations, practitioner groups and artforms mean that competition for available funding has intensified. In addition, arts and cultural policy has been integrated within whole-of-government (or joined up) policy frameworks spanning diverse agencies and policy agendas which, in turn, has served to shape the form of government-sponsored creativity and cultural production (Holden 2004, 2006).

A fracturing of the coherence of the domain of arts and cultural policy has also emerged. Although the traditional arts (opera, ballet, classical music, theatre) have been inscribed formally within the ambit of cultural policy, there is a growing uneasy tension between what counts as 'art' and what counts as 'culture' in terms of how practitioners and administrators view the competing domains and in terms of policy initiatives. Whereas the arts traditionally encompassed cultural practices that were cosseted by social elites (largely through the practices of direct and indirect patronage from private and/or state benefactors), the re-definition of arts policy as cultural policy in the second half of the twentieth century sought to remove the elitist tag from traditional arts *and* include forms of cultural practice that had broad popular appeal (e.g. Australia Council 2000; Hill Strategies 2005c).[1]

This trend was associated with the welfare governance agenda that gave priority to educational, social and quality-of-life outcomes as well as broader democratic and cultural citizenship objectives, such as producing a culturally literate society (cf. Craik, Davis and Sunderland 2000). Arts and culture were accordingly re-defined from strictly educational accompaniments to indicators of the acquisition of social and cultural capital. The broader the definition of culture, the more fragile, incoherent and tension-ridden this policy has become (cf. Craik, McAllister and Davis 2003). The problem becomes where to draw the line as to what counts as culture (and therefore uplifting) and what deserves support. Is an art program run in a hospital to enhance the self-esteem or healing capacity of patients a creative or a medical program? Is digital media training for unemployed youths a creative or a job skilling program? Have arts and culture as welfare been replaced by arts and culture as a social safety net?

Instrumentalism and Sustainability

The instrumental approach to using art and cultural projects to revitalise a sense of community has been around long enough for evaluations to be made. Those in favour of such a strategy emphasise outcomes that have enabled individuals to re-engage with their local community, create a community ethos, improve 'social inclusiveness' and generally promote cultural sustainability. However, even those endorsing instrumental strategies acknowledge that there is a difference between 'good community arts practice' and 'shallow or inauthentic art practices' as well as flaws in evaluation processes that need to be addressed for instrumental arts and cultural projects to be effective (Mulligan 2007: 25, 31). In fact, it is the perceived distinction between art and culture that undermines efforts by government to unify these terms. As community development advocate, Deborah Mills, laments:

> Unfortunately these arguments [about cultural sustainability] do not appear to have been well understood; policy makers often use the terms art and culture synonymously. Perhaps they think that the term *culture might have the broader appeal and help bring the arts in from the margins of government concern*. At other times they appear to be using the term culture as a means of insisting on an opposition between prestige art and community culture. In practice, whatever the policy conception of culture, the actual application of cultural policy by governments is too often reduced to *heritage and the subsidised arts*. Perhaps this is because culture and its role in everyday life are not widely understood in government. (Mills 2007: 36; my italics)

Arguably, attempts to democratise the arts by weakening the bonds of exclusivity practiced by the elite have backfired. The past decade has witnessed a widening schism between 'art' and 'culture'. This is irrespective of whether the policy environment is mired in the old politics of patronage or has promoted alternatives based on marketplace survival. The traditional arts have remained ensconced in a privileged but confined position – lacking in adaptability and administered by niche governmental bureaucracies in the form of specialist agencies (usually through customised cultural statutory authorities or/and government departments). Meanwhile, the rest of cultural policy has been absorbed within whole-of-government approaches across agencies.

Moreover, cultural policy has also become intimately tied up with cultural planning and cultural development (e.g. Florida 2002; Landry and Bianchini 1995; Matarasso 1997). Another advocate of cultural planning, Jon Hawkes (2001), has contributed the idea of culture as one of four *pillars* of sustainability, the others being economic, social and environmental development (cf. Gray 2004, 2006; West and Smith 2005; Merli 2002; Madden and Bloom 2004; Belfiore and Bennett 2006). For cultural development analysts, sustainable development and cultural development are co-dependent. Hawkes (2001: 2, 4) identifies three aspects of 'culture': *values and aspirations* which set the framework of a society's *raison d'être*; *practices and cultural media* through which culture is actualised; and the *visible manifestations and artefacts* of cultural practice.

In this approach to the management of culture, cultural diversity and difference are part-and-parcel of a commitment to cultural sustainability. As part of reconciling cultural sustainability with the other pillars, cultural policy becomes annexed to what I have called elsewhere 'lifestyle culture' or 'eco-culture' (Craik 2005) where art and culture become core planks of cultural planning and everyday 'lived' cultural experiences. The idea of eco-culture encompasses the diverse, ecologically sensitive, globally aware, yet locally responsive culture that characterises everyday civility. Using Walter Benjamin's term, the post-modern citizen is a 'cultural flaneur' in-so-far as s/he exhibits a greater sense of cultural competence and possesses the skills to negotiate complex, and diverse, cultural environments, experiences and forms. Opportunities to partake of cultural experiences have become the *leitmotif* of contemporary life in developed societies. Some commentators have coined the term 'omnivores' to characterise people whose cultural taste 'ranges across genres and forms' (Savage et al. 2005: 6). Should the percentage of cultural omnivores in a society markedly increase then the division between arts and culture and existing modes of supporting and representing art and culture might change significantly.

Reconciling Complex Culture with Cultural Engagement

Yet, the idea of the cultural omnivore has mostly been taken up in support of instrumental uses of culture. The assumptions underlying this are often benign and care-oriented. They are motivated by notions of human improvement. The cultural values on which the notion of cultural sustainability are built stem from a shared consensus of 'core' or 'universal' values that include a wide range of human concerns: participation and democratic rights; tolerance, compassion and inclusion; freedom, justice and equality; peace, safety and security; health, wellbeing and vitality; creativity, imagination and innovation; and even love and respect for the environment (cf. Hawkes 2001: 7). In a similar argument, Jowell (2004) stresses the importance of what she calls *complex culture* and *cultural engagement* (as opposed to simple culture and entertainment) as the means of developing 'personal value' that opens up a 'personal heartland' that enables a person to engage with new ideas, creative forms and cultural possibilities. While this has presented as a new approach to representing the value of culture as a tangible value that governments should recognise and support, her arguments, in many respects, go back to traditional arguments about the value of the arts as a strategy of civility. Indicatively she has argued:

> Public subsidy produces what the market may not sustain — it is almost a bulwark against globalised commercialism that might not be sensitive or responsive to local and national cultural expression. It makes possible what might not otherwise be available, and it makes available the best ... Excellence has to be at the heart of cultural subsidy. (Jowell 2004: par.32-33)

Assumptions that link arts and cultural policy to excellence have persistently underpinned post-WW2 democratic governments (at least rhetorically). Since the 1960s, a second argument about cultural diversity has infiltrated arguments about the arts, yet has played second fiddle and generally referred to benign and non-threatening forms of culture. It is arguable that such assumptions have been challenged by the onslaught of security concerns, terrorism and non-Western ideologies that have dominated recent preoccupations about culture and humanity. Unquestioned regard for western forms of democratic rights and human rights has been severely tested, especially by Islamic extremism. Diversity, most spectacularly in the form of multiculturalism, is under threat from cultural assumptions that challenge the belief that tolerance and inclusive policies can iron out clashes between radically different values, norms and behaviours. Has the clamour for universal rights and international declarations faded? Are they relevant in this new cultural climate? There has been a shift from the late twentieth century approach to cultural policy and its tenets of diversity and development to recognition of the perceived 'threat' of cultural difference, separatism and forceful rejection of the idea of cultural and inclusive and multi-dimensional. The question we need to ask is 'how should governments respond to this new cultural agenda and the fallout from the ongoing re-alignment of power and culture?'

One response to this situation has, paradoxically, been increased insularity of traditional 'arts' policy — restrictive, elitist and clientelist. This is partly because the lobbyists for cultural policy have largely come from the arts sector and focused on familiar arts forms as strategies to enhance cultural development. At the same time, the re-definition of cultural policy as cultural (or creative) industry policy and the emphasis on economic benefits and potential of culture to be sustainable — even profitable — has shaped emergent forms of cultural policy. Culture, usually arts and heritage, become implicated in the quest for sustainability although the bulk of support still is directed towards high end capital 'C' culture.

Despite the development of new approaches to cultural policy and arts funding through the twentieth century, the persistence of an artistic hierarchy[2] underpinning the policy sector has meant that at times of crisis and change, culture has reverted to 'Art' at each phase while culture has been given a broadbrush treatment as a panacea for insoluble social itches and uncomfortable truths. Rather than embracing major changes in cultural participation, education and consumption as the cornerstone of arts and cultural policy, the sector remains on the backburner of subsidy.

ENDNOTES

[1] Examples include contemporary dance, digital arts, new media, community cultural practice, youth arts, circus or physical arts, architecture, fashion and indigenous cultural practice.

[2] An example of the exclusiveness of the cultural lobby's aesthetic hierarchy was evident following the death of the highly popular artist, Pro Hart, in 2006. Although 'a runaway commercial success', not a single Pro Hart painting was in a state or national gallery collection. A parallel was drawn with L.S. Lowry's struggle 'to gain institutional and critical acceptance' (Smee 2006: 21). The curator of Australian art at the Art Gallery of NSW explained: 'Art galleries are elitist in the best sense. They try to collect the greatest artists, the ones whose works will have meaning over time. Pro, very early in his career, discovered a language, a voice that became very popular. It was very formulaic, but it brought pleasure to many people. But it's rather like comparing Slim Dusty to Mozart. There's nothing wrong with Slim Dusty's music. It just has a different appeal; it's a voice of the people.' Yet, as Smee observed, 'there are mediocre works galore in every state and national collection in Australia. Many of them are on permanent display.' After a flurry of debate about whether Hart's status as an 'outsider' was warranted,

curators modified their position. One described him as 'one of the most delightful illustrators of the Australian folk idiom, but let's not use the word art anywhere' (quoted by Sexton 2006: 10). Although some galleries have subsequently (and reluctantly one suspects) acquired token works by Hart, the nub of the problem remains that Pro Hart was too popular and appealed to 'the average Aussie'. As the former One Nation politician Pauline Hanson noted, 'I suppose we are in the same boat, because the elites of the political world never accepted me either'.

Chapter 4: International trends in arts and cultural production and consumption

The re-visioning of arts and cultural policy has occurred to varying degrees across the international stage. Partly, this has been in response to trends in cultural participation and consumption, as well as changing approaches to strategies of support. In particular, a number of trends are characterised by trade-offs between the following factors:

- the ability to be financially self-sufficient or non-reliant on government largesse;
- the ratio between the costs of cultural practice and production, and ability to generate revenue;
- the size and market profile of audiences and consumers of arts and culture; and
- the degree of cross-form transformations of cultural practice.

Cultural Consumption

When these relationships are investigated, it is clear that artistic and cultural forms that rely most heavily on government support are those that are least popular. Moreover, these are the artforms consumed by audiences with the greatest capacity to purchase the culture they desire, namely, that segment of the population with high incomes and high cultural capital (and who are older, more likely to be female and live in inner-city areas). Conversely, those artistic and cultural forms that rely least on government support are consumed in greater quantity, are more likely to have a mixed consumer base and tend to offer greater choice (Australia Council 2000; 2003; Hill Strategies 2005c; Keane 2004; Lee 2004). Cross-cultural comparisons show similar patterns (e.g. Mandel (2006) on cultural participation in Germany).

Consumer spending on cultural goods and services in developed countries has increased, in aggregate terms, by almost half in less than a decade. A closer look at expenditure data reveals, however, that a significant proportion of spending has been concentrated on the consumption of books, live performing arts (broadly defined), and admission to museums and heritage sites/national parks/botanic gardens. The most popular cultural goods and services are movies and DVDs, popular music and CDs, street markets and community fêtes, festivals, and art/craft hobbies. Without incentives, only a minority of ordinary people choose to spend money on traditional arts and culture. Yet, despite the low demand, the number of professional artists has more than tripled over the same period.

In other words, there is a dramatic over-supply of cultural practitioners particularly in the least popular cultural forms (meaning, these practitioners have low incomes and contingent earnings).

The rationale of provision rather than consumption has supposedly been endorsed by statistics showing that people generally support cultural venues whether or not they are themselves customers. As one might expect, and customers might know, libraries are the most supported cultural facilities. Museums, performing arts venues and art galleries are supported to a lesser extent. While support certainly increases with use, only a minority of non-users support the need for generous government support for culture as a broad category. At best, statistics on usage have been used to justify continued funding for art and culture. But when we look at patterns of cultural consumption they show that people continue to prefer 'popular' cultural activities to 'high culture' ones.

Australia

Australians typify this pattern, consuming, in rank order of preference: cinema, botanic gardens and libraries, followed by animal and marine parks.[1] Way below come museums, popular music concerts, and opera or musicals. At the bottom end of consumption come other performing arts, theatre, dance and classical music concerts (Craik, Davis & Sunderland 2000: 194).

Moreover, as the *Nugent Report* (DCITA 1999: 199-200) found, the development of new forms of performing arts — musical spectaculars, festivals, opera and dance spectaculars — as well as film forms, DVDs and CDs — has provided 'intense competition' for traditional performing arts, especially opera and dance. However, a review of the major performing arts companies in 2003 (MPAB 2004) found that — despite an extensive rescue package with guaranteed ongoing funding, management support, more touring, more paid audience revenue, more new works and greater sponsorship — aggregate losses have increased by 74% over the period of review, suggesting a dramatic decline in their financial position and likely viability.

Yet, when we focus on 'who should pay' for cultural activities and organisations, familiar arguments are still used to justify continued government underwriting of the high end of the arts and cultural sector. The classic 'special pleading' position to justify supporting the least sustainable forms of culture is a mixture of arguments about the need to support forms of cultural excellence, maintain international competitiveness and enrich national culture. As the above analysis indicates, such arguments depend on a hierarchy of art and cultural forms where the least viable are located at the top of the pecking order despite being the most marginal in terms of popularity. This should prompt a radical rethink of the philosophy of arts and cultural policy. So, what realistic alternatives are available?

Canada

A Canadian study, for example, analysed expenditure on books compared with expenditure on other cultural items, revealing that Canadian households are high cultural spenders:

> The $1.1 billion spent on books is fairly similar to overall spending on newspapers ($1.2 billion) and movie theatre admissions ($1.2 billion) and amounts to more than double the spending on live sporting events ($451 million). (Hill Strategies 2005a: 2)

In all, 63% of Canadian households spent money on newspapers, 61% of households on movie theatres, 54% of households bought magazines and 48% of households purchased books. Households were much less likely to spend money on 'art, antiques and decorative ware' (only 29% of households), on 'live performing arts' (36% of households), or on 'admission to museums' (32% of households). And only 19% of households bought tickets for 'live sports events' (Hill Strategies 2005a: 2).

Of the book buyers, there appears to be a relationship between high expenditure on books and expenditure on other cultural activities (performing arts, museums, art/craft and live sports). This appears to demonstrate that a high level of cultural consumption provides an indicator of high cultural capital (Hill Strategies 2005a) thus adding support to the concept of 'cultural omnivore' mentioned earlier. Moreover, high cultural spenders have the following distinctive demographic and lifestyle characteristics: they have high incomes, they are middle aged, they are twice as likely to have no children, four times as likely to have no teenagers, and live in a one or two-person dwelling. High cultural spenders are also most likely to be homeowners and live in large cities.

These figures show that expenditure on books is a good indicator of overall cultural expenditure: 'high spenders on books have much higher spending on other arts, entertainment and sporting items [including children's camps, sporting equipment, toys, games and hobbies, and photographic goods or services] than non-spenders' (Hill Strategies 2005a: 12). These figures are similar to research in the United States that showed that:

> Book lovers tend to frequent a number of different types of arts and sporting activities. In fact, arts museum and performing arts attendance were found to be 'significant factors in literature participation, even adjusting for education, ethnicity, race and other factors'. (Hill Strategies 2005a: 12)

In sum, '76% of highest-income households spent some money on books, compared with 23% of lowest-income households' yet 'the financial commitment required to buy books is much more significant for low-income households than for high-income households' (20). The figures on book-buying illustrate the selective and elitist nature of cultural consumption and the policies underlying cultural policy. Financial well-being is an important factor in cultural consumption. So too are educational levels, cultural and social capital, normative household structure and locational profile. Given that books are one of the more highly consumed cultural products within a population, it is possible to extrapolate even more skewed consumer profiles for other arts/cultural forms.

These observations are consistent with Savage et al. (2005) in their study of cultural capital in the United Kingdom which found that, despite new cultural forms and wider opportunities for cultural consumption, there were 'marked patterns of differentiation in tastes, many of which appear familiar from long term historical patterns' that confirm the correlation between high cultural capital and wealth and education. This evidence, to some extent, challenges the proposition that cultural omnivores are transforming patterns of cultural consumption (cf. Peterson and Kern 1996).

One of the movers and shakers in the nexus between cultural policy and planning in recent times has been Richard Florida (2002, 2005) who has attempted to establish a link between the cultural indicators exhibited by a community or locality and measures of quality of life and wealth. He has contended that city and regional economies facing economic pressures and de-industrialisation should look to establishing cultural industries to spearhead a revitalisation. To this end, Florida developed the 'Bohemian index' as a measure of high 'cultural competence' against economic potential and well-being. This model has received international acclaim yet its assertions have largely been untested. In one of the few studies that has attempted to evaluate this model, Hill Strategies (2005b) compared 'the bohemian index ranking with two indicators of cultural spending in 15 Canadian metropolitan areas: per capita cultural spending and per capita spending on art works and events'. They concluded that:

> Overall, it appears that the cultural occupations variable (bohemian index) and the two spending indicators do not follow a consistent pattern. Victoria, Calgary and Ottawa rank fairly high on all three indicators, but the largest metropolitan areas — Toronto, Montreal and Vancouver — rank higher on the bohemian index than on the spending indicators. The reverse is true for Edmonton and Regina, areas that rank higher on the cultural spending data than on the cultural occupations data' (Hill Strategies 2005b: 9).

Creative Economies

Nonetheless, as Cunningham (2006: 17) notes, Florida 'has highlighted the wider economic significance of creative human capital [by correlating] population diversity, high-tech output, innovation and human capital'. According to Florida's index, 'Global Sydney', 'Melbourne Inner' and the Australian Capital

Territory are the most creative and internationally competitive locales in Australia. For his own part, Cunningham has developed a 'creative trident' measure of:

> ... creative occupations within the creative industries ('specialist'), plus the creative occupations employed in *other* industries ('embedded'), plus the *support* occupations employed in creative industries. (Cunningham 2006: 20)

On this basis, the number of creative practitioners and the calculation of the contribution of creative activity to the Australian economy is far greater that official figures show, suggesting that there is greater potential for creative work to be recognised as part of the overall economy than is currently the case.

Detailed studies, such as these, need to be replicated in other countries and cities in order to test many of the assumptions underpinning contemporary arts and cultural policy. At a macro level, there is a need to interrogate levels of government spending on arts and culture via international comparisons and to examine the emerging forms of support for art and culture (cf. Florida 2005). Despite difficulties in making international comparisons (Madden 2004), McCaughey (2005) has attempted to compare Canada with other countries in terms of arts funding. Despite Mark Schuster's cautionary note that 'countries with smaller populations will have higher per capita expenditures because of their difference in size, not their difference in policy' (quoted by McCaughey 2005: 3), figures show that in the Northern European states and Britain, expenditure per capita is much higher than in British settler states (Australia, New Zealand, Canada and Singapore) and that all are much higher that the United States. Countries with small populations seem more likely to commit to cultural funding than those with large populations.

It is also interesting to examine the operation and performance of different funding models. Countries with direct government funding, as opposed to arms' length funding (via arts councils), tend to spend considerably more on culture. This suggests that countries (and governments) who adopt an 'architect' or 'engineer' approach to arts and culture have made the arts and culture a higher policy priority than governments who have adopted more 'hands off' nurturer or facilitator approaches. Where mixed policy models are adopted, such as elite nurturer or parameter-shaping models, higher relative expenditure on arts and culture can be shown.

Overall, McCaughey's study reveals a gulf between governments who regard arts and culture as a *core* priority for government policy and expenditure (e.g. Germany, Netherlands, Austria, France and Scandinavia) and those for whom it is a footnote or *marginal* responsibility (Canada, Australia, New Zealand, Singapore and Switzerland). There is clearly an historical element here. Countries with a long tradition of supporting arts and culture have maintained support at substantially higher levels. However, even in countries with long traditions of generous government support, there is an emerging crisis as governments pull out of longstanding commitments. The arts and cultural sectors have been pushed to seek alternate sources of funding, such as sponsorships and partnerships, even in countries like Germany (Hausmann 2006), Italy (Comunian 2006), Austria (Hunjet 2006), Scandinavia (Lindqvist 2006), the Netherlands (Segers 2006) and Japan (Kobayashi 2006). Countries in the former eastern block are similarly affected (Obuljen 2006).

Although there is evidence that these strategies have produced the sought-after responses, there appear to be limits to the potential for an expansion of private support and the kinds of cultural organisations or activities sponsors will invest in. There also appears to be a clear relationship between the economic prosperity of a nation and the likelihood of securing sponsorship (Segers 2006; Lindqvist 2006). Concomitantly, there is less evaluation of the efficacy of expenditure in the higher-funding countries than in those where cultural support is regarded as a budgetary footnote or extravagance.

What does this mean for current trends internationally in arts and cultural support and likely futures? While traditional forms of arts and cultural support have persisted, they have been required to adapt to new conditions of governance, globalisation and changing patterns of cultural consumption which has, in turn, created acute challenges for arts and cultural policy making.

ENDNOTES

[1] A study of cultural participation by the Australian Bureau of Statistics in 2002 showed that annual cultural consumption by Australians occurs in cascading proportions: the most popular are cinema (69.9%); libraries (42.1%); botanic gardens (41.6%); and zoological gardens (40%). Next come popular music (26.4%); other museums (25%); art museums and galleries (24.9%; and other performing arts (20.4%). Less than one in five Australians attend music and opera (18.7%) or theatre (18.0%) and only one in 10 attend dance (10.9%) or classical music (9%) (ABS 2004b).

Chapter 5: How can cultural sub-sectors respond? Three indicative case studies

This chapter examines some sub-sectors that have challenged prevailing policy approaches to the management of culture. We have already explored the plight of performing arts in the contemporary policy context. It was suggested that the management of performing arts entities had been buffeted by the key debates and issues in the arena of arts and cultural policy including: access and equity; audience development; community cultural development; cultural diversity; indigenous cultural production; national versus local culture; globalisation and cultural export; elite versus popular culture; electronic transformations of culture; and youth arts.

In the following pages I briefly explore several *micro-studies* of specific cultural sub-sectors: *museums*; *indigenous arts and culture*; and *circus*. These have been chosen because of the extent to which they challenge orthodox characterisations of — as well as contemporary approaches to policy-making for — the arts and cultural sector. The first study, on *museums*, examines the 'crisis' in the new 'museology'. The second, on *indigenous arts and culture*, explores an area that has evolved from a marginal ethnographic interest into a major plank in national cultural policy and, moreover, has succeeded in balancing government support with commercial success. The third case study examines *circus*, which, as an 'outsider' genre, challenges many of the assumptions underpinning policy governing the mainstream arts and cultural sectors by developing an innovative and vibrant new artform that has revolutionised ideas about performance, spectacle, physical training, cultural export and audience development.

Micro-study of museums

Museums are a vexed area of cultural policy. In the West, museums developed partly as a consequence of European exploration and the collection of artefacts, natural objects and material culture from 'exotic' lands, places and peoples (Bennett 1995; Hooper-Greenhill 1995; Bennett, Trotter & McAlear 1996; Horne 1984; National Museum of Australia 2006). This coincided with the development of modern science and theories of evolution where a classificatory and taxonomic mentality structured the curation of collections into so-called 'cabinets of curiosity'.

Traditional museums presented their collections in regimented displays of similar and different things, carefully identified by scientific names and classificatory details. The importance of museums paralleled the emergence in the nineteenth century of public institutions designed to support the development of modern notions of citizenship and democracy, education and enlightenment. Museums were 'temples' of auto-didacticism and pedagogy, rich resources of exotic objects and knowledge about 'other-ness' that fed into European notions of civility and the conquest of 'primitive' worlds.

But the fascination with displays of Egyptian mummies, dinosaur bones, taxonomies of butterflies, indigenous weapons, fishing equipment, fauna and flora, shrunken skulls and extinct and endangered animals and skeletons waned considerably during the twentieth century. By the 1960s, museums were regarded as dark, dusty, musty places filled with relics of the past. Museums were suddenly in crisis! The public was no longer enthralled and enchanted by such displays. A debate ensued about the purpose of museums, how they ought to be financed and who was their natural audience.

Why did museums exist? The earlier rationale of collection and curation was challenged by new approaches to knowledge and learning and a partial rejection of classificatory approaches to knowing about the world and the past. Critics demanded a modern political interpretation of objects and contextualisation of museum collections. The purpose of holding huge collections of objects was questioned and the cost of storage, curation and display became an issue. In particular, commentators and critics questioned why governments should pay to keep open expensive, unpopular cultural institutions that few wanted to visit and many found unsatisfying? Busloads of dragooned school children made up a good proportion of museum visitors but generally discretionary visitors were few and far between even when entry was free.

Critiques of museology in the 1970s generated a push for new approaches to museums that endorsed a reflexive approach to history and civilisation. Henceforward, museums would engage critical discourses addressing issues of race, class, colonisation, power relations and empowerment (van Oost 2006). Instead of simply looking at objects of history and presenting one (didactic) point of view to a passive audience, it was argued that museums should offer diverse perspectives and present material in ways that visitors could engage with in a *hands-on* interactive way. The new museums focused on national and cultural identities and difference as much as natural history and experimented with presenting 'living history' and aspects of everyday life and culture instead of the earlier focus on official and scientific perspectives. The result was a combination of new interpretive strategies and interactive exhibits, often using new technologies and active participation. The new museum became a place of entertainment where learning should take place through enjoyment not didacticism. 'Thrills' were built into experiential displays (such as real earthquake simulations, robotic dinosaurs, participatory re-creations of long-gone customs such as traditional classrooms and interactive digital 'games').

New museums were concerned with the environment, community, cultural diversity and the political shaping of culture. Inevitably, such museums were perceived as politicised, no longer just displaying things in a 'neutral' way but engaging with political debates and changing perspectives. Museums were expected to develop outreach programs (e.g. become part of visitor sightseeing schedules, appoint experts in residence, offer vacation programs for children, develop community projects with special interest groups, etc.) that engaged with their communities, digitalise collections and make them accessible to visitors (actual and virtual) and build new audiences. The emphasis was firmly on making museums entertaining spaces. The new museum was a kind of theme park.[1]

These changes have had critical significance for the funding and management of museums. Rather than depending on recurrent funding by government and scientific bodies, museums have been pushed into finding new sponsors and develop corporate, research and commercial partnerships. Managers, administrators, marketing staff, educational staff and volunteer guides have replaced the traditional staffing profile of museums with curators and scientists at the fore. But like hospitals and schools, museums rarely have professional managers and the 'scientific' faction versus the 'educational' faction often dominates internal politics. Curators tend to be the least heard group in the contemporary museum and are often employed on a contract basis. The value of storing collections away, hiding things that no-one ever gets to see, remains a sore point in museum management. A few museums, such as the Museum of Civilisation in Canada, have an open access storage facility where visitors themselves can explore the collection. Most museums however have warehouses full of 'stuff' well out of the public's reach.

Funding remains an issue. Recurrent funding and block grants have been replaced by project funding and case funding. Internally, the lion's share of the budget now goes on administration with tiny amounts on curating and mounting new exhibitions. Research sections are under-funded and oriented towards in-house research rather than research through public engagement. Partnership arrangements can be successful but are often project-specific or unstable (annual or short-term arrangements) and they fluctuate depending on levels of popular interest and prevailing economic conditions.

It is also important to distinguish different kinds of museums and their financial needs and arrangements. Each has a specific profile that shapes performance and viability.

To name some, these include: national museums (National Museum of Australia, Te Papa, Museum of Civilisation); living history museums (Skansen in Stockholm, Sovereign Hill in Ballarat, Colonial Williamsburg in Virginia); community museums (Jondaryan in Queensland — home of the famous shearers' strike, Tambo Museum in Queensland — known for its teddy bears, Whitby Museum in Northeast Yorkshire — known for the mummified 'hand of glory'); specialist museums (maritime museums; Victoria and Albert Museum, London; portrait galleries); art museums (the Guggenheim Museums in New York and Biboa; the Getty Museum in Los Angeles); industrial museums (Ironbridge in the Severn Gorge, England; the Ipswich Railway Museum in Queensland); cultural heritage museums (Head-Smashed-In Buffalo Jump in Alberta); social history museums (Hanseatic Museum in Bergen; Viking Museum in York; Nederlands Openluchtmuseum in Arnhem); technological museums (Powerhouse Museum in Sydney, MAK in Vienna, Ars Electronica Center in Linz; Global Arts Link, Ipswich, Queensland); science museums (Questacon in Canberra); natural history museums (The Smithsonian; La Brea Tar Pits in Los Angeles); museums of antiquity (The Pergamon Museum in Berlin, the British Museum in London); and so on.

Museums pose significant problems for cultural policy since there is significant infrastructure to maintain, costly collections, political accountability as well as specific issues associated with management, display and visitation. Since the retreat from automatic state patronage of major cultural institutions, no simple solution has emerged to effectively manage the museum sector.

The poignant story of the 'crisis' of the National Museum of Australia highlights these dilemmas. Talked about since 1928, and reactivated by the Pigott Report in 1975 (Report of the Committee of Inquiry on Museums and National Collections 1975), the NMA finally opened in 2001 on the banks of Lake Burley Griffin in Canberra. Given its new-ness, the NMA was never conceived as a monument to the past and scientific collections, rather it was intended to reflect Australia's 'contemporary mood of nationalism' by 'capturing the plurality of knowledge and experience of its people' (McCarthy 2004).

The building, designed in the shape of a rainbow serpent, was far smaller than originally envisaged and, although its collection was small, it could not accommodate more than a fraction of the objects in its collection. The establishment of the NMA as a national cultural institution was at odds with dominant government ideology in a number of respects, particularly in its rejection of 'the Howard government's celebratory position on Australian history and national identity … and modernist-linear … interpretation' of Australian history (McCarthy 2004). What should a national collection consist of? Should it be housed in a single building? How should it display and make accessible its collection? How should it relate to national identity?

The NMA chose to organise its collection around three themes — land, nation and people — and use interactive and digital technology, where possible, to engage visitors. It also stressed the diversity of Australia's population, in particular, emphasising indigenous culture and peoples (Casey 1999). This led to a government-led attack on the institution accusing it of presenting a 'black armband view of history' resulting in the departure of the inaugural (indigenous) director, Dawn Casey, and prompting a re-evaluation of the role and form of the museum (Carroll report 2005; Review of the National Museum of Australia 2005).

The review rejected the NMA's pluralist version of Australian history and called for a 'consensus' account that emphasised the Australian characteristics of 'inclusiveness, a 'fair-go' ethos, a distrust of extremisms and civic common sense' (Review of the NMA 2003:4). This amounted to presenting a 'celebratory narrative' of Australia centred on the figure of Captain James Cook and downplaying the colonial struggles and conflict between indigenous Australians and European settlers (McCarthy 2004). Mc Carthy concludes that:

> The NMA was to be a dialogue between nation and national identity. The political dilemma came when this dialogue became pluralist: wanting to include people's history, being postmodernist in the architecture and post-colonial in its indigenous sensibilities. All three influences challenged the agenda of the Howard government. Pluralism was a threat because it was associated with diversity and multiculturalism. Postmodernism was a threat because it challenged the government's claims of linear advancement under the neo-liberal agenda. Post-colonialism was a threat because it not only raised the whole character of settler history but also pointed to the on-going plight of the indigenous people as a result of their dispossession. For all these reasons, the attack on the NMA was sustained and successful in stifling dissent.

This episode demonstrates the inherent fragility of the new museology under current governance arrangements in which cultural institutions are subject to the government's dominant political orthodoxy via appointed boards of management.

Micro-study of indigenous arts and cultural policy

As in many other advanced countries, the role of indigenous culture in mainstream cultural policy has increased significantly in recent years. Australia, Canada, South Africa and New Zealand typify those countries with a colonial history, where a diverse indigenous culture has in recent years been re-discovered and its value revised. In Australia, the elements of traditional indigenous culture include music, dance, art and craft, Dreamtime stories and life survival stories (Queensland Cultural Tourism Framework 1996).

In addition, new forms of artistic and cultural expression of indigenous culture have emerged. While this trend has been closely associated with issues of indigenous identity, self-determination and economic independence, the recent *renaissance* of indigenous culture has also been important in revising notions of national identity and national culture. This revival has spawned a raft of inquiries into how best to manage and support the indigenous cultural industry (including the ATSIC Cultural Policy Framework 1995; Draft National Aboriginal and Torres Strait Islander Cultural Industry Strategy 1994; ATSIC and the Office of Tourism National Aboriginal and Torres Strait Islander Tourism Industry Strategy 1997).

Indigenous culture has become an iconic flagship in the promotion of Australia's cultural specificity and difference. Indigenous cultural themes are used extensively in tourism promotion, for example, and indigenous art has been exhibited and artists celebrated internationally. The ATSI arts industry is estimated to be worth over $200 million annually and growing by 10% per annum. For example, in 1998-99, sales of ATSI arts and crafts in the Northern Territory alone accounted for $48.7 million and in 1997 Australian households spent $70.8 million on ATSI arts and crafts. Half of expenditure on the arts by international tourists is spent on ATSI arts and crafts ($77.7m out of $147.5m) (Altman and Taylor 1990; ATSIC 1994; ATSIC 1995; ATSIC & Office of Tourism 1997; ABS 2004).

Indigenous culture has also been important in creating employment opportunities for indigenous people with dance, choreography and visual arts occupations having the highest ATSI employment among cultural occupations. In all, there are 5,000-6,000 practising ATSI artists and craftspeople.

The emergence of an ATSI arts and craft genre was driven, initially, by government supported programs and projects. Important milestones include Geoffrey Bardon's introduction of acrylic paints to the community of Papunya in the 1970s (Bardon 1979; Helmrich 2003; Bardon and Bardon 2004); the Utopia movement with the introduction of screen printing and, later, works on canvas in the 1980s; and the emergence in the mid-1990s of the Lockhart River Art Gang with its vibrant mix of traditional and contemporary genres (Neales 2002; BAM 2003; QAG 2003). Numerous Western desert communities now also have thriving arts centres producing highly distinctive paintings, prints and crafts as shown in the *skin to skin* exhibition as part of NAIDOC 2007 (Tuggeranong Arts Centre 2007). As always, there was a mixture of motives with welfare, employment and training, community building and improved health outcomes to the fore rather than simply promoting culture for its own sake. Once established, the market tended to be driven by metropolitan galleries and collectors and the international art market as well as international visitors (Mundine 2005).

Indigenous art offers diverse artforms and cultural activities including: visual arts (works on canvas, printmaking, bark, ceramics); crafts (revived traditional crafts and new ones — wood objects and carving, basket weaving, beads and seeds, sculpture, jewellery, clothing, fabric screen printing, weaving and knitting); indigenous cultural performances; cultural centres and *keeping places*; indigenous cultural heritage displays and cultural tours; and indigenous cultural festivals. The latter include the Laura, Aboriginal Dance and Torres Strait Festival in Townsville; the Croc (anti-drug) Festival on Thursday Island in the Torres Strait; the Stompem Ground in Broome, Western Australia; the Garma Festival in Arnhem Land in the Northern Territory; Survival; and the Alice Springs Beanie Festival in the Northern Territory.

Indigenous cultural production, distribution and consumption have a number of distinctive features, including:

- debates over traditional styles and techniques versus new ones (e.g. the use of acrylic paints, non-traditional colours, contemporary images and genres, new and multi-media);
- the legitimacy of 'urban' indigenous artists addressing contemporary themes, versus 'bush' artists with their focus on traditional indigenous culture;
- distinctive website commerce — leading the arts community in selling via the internet;
- belated recognition by major auction houses that have massively inflated the price of indigenous artworks;
- the popularity of commissioned work;
- issues of intellectual property rights over cultural products; and
- partial integration with indigenous cultural tourism and cultural heritage activities.

At the same time that indigenous culture has expanded as a sector, a number of pressing issues have emerged specific to this form of culture. Five key issues for ATSI cultural development were identified at an ATSIS[2] Vision Day (Australia Council Aboriginal and Torres Strait Islander Fund 2000):

1. The need to protect indigenous cultural and intellectual property (Johnson 1996, 1999).[3] This includes the unauthorised use of Aboriginal motifs and designs in clothing or interior décor.[4] A number of attempts have been made to produce a 'Label of Authenticity' and copyright arrangements for royalty payments and re-use of work. A particular issue is that or 'authorship'. Unlike Western artistic traditions, much indigenous work is produced collectively often under the guidance or instruction of the key artist leading to claims that works have been sold and awards given inappropriately to single artists rather than a group.[5]
2. The need to increase visibility of indigenous arts both in Australia and internationally. This concerns how best to market and promote indigenous culture — and by whom.[6]
3. The need to increase economic and cultural sustainability — most money from indigenous cultural consumption goes to middlemen, not to indigenous producers. Where individuals are paid, an individual is expected to distribute the money through their family members, often leaving little for the individual producer. European gatekeepers are also significant in

deciding who and what should be supported and promoted (Rothwell 2006; Ryan 2006).

4. The need for Indigenous people to manage and determine their own arts practices — Indigenous cultural centres and companies have had mixed fortunes and still often reliant on go-betweens. Examples of best practice include the Fire-works Gallery in Brisbane and its Camp Fire group of artists that supports grass roots artistic production; the Art Gang Exhibition from the Lockhart River Art and Cultural Centre in Cape York put this locality on the map as a dynamic emerging new arts centre; and the fibre art practice of the women of Western Arnhem Land (BAM 2003; QAG 2003; Hamby 2005).

5. The need to increase indigenous participation in non-indigenous festivals and events — arguments concern the danger of tokenism and ghettoisation; the challenge of reaching wider mainstream Australian audiences; and increasing public awareness and acceptance of indigenous culture and issues. Theatrical performances such as Deborah Mailman's play 'The Seven Stages of Grieving' (co-written by Enoch Wesley) have been important in getting such issues raised on a wider public issue agenda (McCallum 2002: 14).

Indigenous cultural success stories include the internationally acclaimed contemporary indigenous dance company, Bangarra Dance Theatre, the leading; Tjapukai Cultural Centre in Cairns which combines cultural performance with cultural heritage and indigenous cultural and language training; the popular music group Yothu Yindi; television star and role model Ernie Dingo; and internationally successful visual artists.[7]

What are the consequences of the success of contemporary Indigenous artists for reconceptualising the arts and culture policy domain? Indigenous culture has challenged many of the scenarios of arts and cultural policy. Although initially subsumed within a suite of 'welfare' and redistribution policies, the sector has become entwined with issues of self-determination, political activism, rejection of mainstream governance, pan-indigeneity (linking Aboriginal culture with other indigenous groups), professionalisation and commercial potential.

Increasing concern about exploitation in the indigenous arts and crafts sector had been the subject of journalistic investigation by *The Australian* newspaper and had also been detailed in a report to the Australia Council (Janke and Quiggin 2006). Issues included payment of royalties, copyright, lack of appropriate remuneration to artists, and unethical practices ('sweatshops', paying in alcohol, non-indigenous reproductions, forgeries, fakes, unscrupulous 'middle-men') (see, for example, Rothwell 2006; Janke and Quiggin 2006; Australia Council 2007 Attachment 2). These revelations eventually led to the establishment of the *Senate inquiry into Australia's Indigenous visual arts and craft sector*, chaired by West Australian Liberal Senator Alan Eggleston, to investigate and identify 'strategies and mechanisms to strengthen the sector' and 'build a more sustainable Indigenous arts industry' (Kemp 2006). In particular, the committee was charged with investigating 'unscrupulous and unethical conduct that occurs in the sector' (Kemp 2006; Senate Standing Committee on the Environment, Communications, Information Technology and the Arts 2006; Arts Hub 2006). The report of the inquiry — *Indigenous Art — Securing the Future; Australia's Indigenous visual arts and craft sector* — published in June 2007, recommended the establishment of an indigenous art industry code of conduct. The inquiry also recommended the indigenous arts industry be given two years to self-regulate or face having a code of conduct prescribed under the *Trade Practices Act* (Dow, 2007; Senate Standing Committee on Environment, Communications, Information Technology and the Arts, 2007).

Increasingly, too, indigenous culture — and international awareness of its importance — has driven national cultural agendas as expressed in national performances (such as the Sydney Olympics opening ceremony, cultural tourism programs, international expositions and exhibitions). Also, indigenous themes have infused all forms of cultural production, whether by indigenous or non-indigenous artists. For a sub-sector that was perceived to reply on patronage models of support, indigenous culture has confounded assumptions underpinning all aspects of Australian cultural policy. However, these recommendations are directed towards the output end of indigenous art rather than the fragile sustainability of the art centres and the cultural context of indigenous art production — especially in remote communities (Rothwell 2007: 16).

Micro-study of circus[8]

We have noted a tension between funding for traditional performing arts and an emerging preference for cultural infrastructure and community-based events. Like youth art (also called slash art because of its propensity to mix artforms), events such as festivals and circuses can challenge existing funding categories, raising awkward questions for government about the basis for funding some artistic forms but not others. The recent rise of circus as an artform has especially challenged aesthetic hierarchies and cultural support models. It offers an exciting form of spectacle, has been hugely popular with audiences on a global scale, provides training in physical arts and cultural performance that appeals to children and adults alike, and — above all — is immensely profitable (Drinnan 2001). Perhaps not surprisingly, circus has been re-cast as 'physical arts'.

Circuses are an age-old phenomenon that seemed to be dying out when, in 1984, Canadian Guy Laiberte established *Cirque du Soleil*. The company developed the idea of 'new circus' or 'physical theatre', combining the physical feats and danger of circus performances with a dramatic sense of spectacle and characterisation.

Cirque du Soleil enjoyed immediate success and spawned circus arts programs throughout North America, in many cases supplanting traditional physical education and sports programs because it was so popular.

The company now has up to six troupes touring constantly all over the world, employing 500 creative artists as well as engaging in extensive marketing, training and franchising activities. To avoid the problem of different quality venues in different places, Cirque du Soleil has developed its own demountable *Grand Chapiteau* (Big Top) that seats 2,500 people and provides all the necessary facilities (bar, restaurant, toilets, cloakroom, shop, etc.). Over 60 million people worldwide have seen a *Cirque du Soleil* performance, a figure beyond the wildest dreams of traditional performing arts organisations. In 2007 alone, 8 million people are expected to attend a show (http://www.cirquedusoleil.com/CirqueDuSoleil/en/Pressroom/cirquedusoleil/factsheets/cds.glance.htm).

Success has encouraged many practitioners and audiences back to the artform. In Australia, companies such as *Circus Oz*, the *Flying Fruit Fly Circus*, *Rock 'n' Roll Circus* and *Vulcana Women's Circus* have experienced a resurgence in funding, audiences and performance (Strickland 1999). Along with active circus companies, many training programs keep alive the physical skills of the art. Though initially suspicious of circus culture, governments are now eager to fund companies and support dedicated training academies such as the National Institute of Circus Arts in Melbourne, established in 1995. It has also attracted generous private sponsorship: for example, the global management consultancy, the Empower Group, sponsored *Circus Oz*, in the process, winning a 2003 AbaF Award (Brown 2003).

In circus, governments see not just a popular artform but possibilities for touring and exports — though such support brings a danger of over-supply with audiences eventually tiring of the spectacle circus offers. Circus has been an unexpected winner amid overall gloom in the cultural sector. Indeed, *Circus Oz* was one of the few companies identified by the *Nugent Report* as being 'successful', in good financial health and having opportunities to win international audiences. Circus shows that some performing arts can flourish outside traditional institutional structures. That very success allows circus to challenge other artforms for access to government funding.

These case studies illustrate the complexities of dealing with the diverse sub-sectors of arts and culture under a single policy framework. As argued elsewhere (Craik, McAlister and Davis 2003) incoherence and contradiction in adjacent policy strategies may be an increasingly distinctive component of policies for this sector.

ENDNOTES

[1] In 2002, just over a third of adult Australians had visited a museum in the past year (men 33.2%) and women (37.5%) with attendance peaking between the 1930s and early 1960s. Half of the attendees came only once, and a quarter twice. 60% of entries were free (ABS 2004a).

[2] ATSIS — the Aboriginal and Torres Strait Islander Services — was the funding arm of the former Aboriginal and Torres Strait Islander Commission (ATSIC). It was abolished on 1 July 2004 and its functions distributed to mainstream agencies.

[3] Some have been taken up as court cases, including the first $1 dollar note designed by David Malangi for the Reserve Bank for which he was paid a $1,000 ex-gratia payment plus a fishing kit and a silver medallion; Flash T-shirts, which used reproductions of the designs of Johnny Bulun Bulun without permission (1989); and the Aboriginal carpet case (Banduk Marika V Indofurn 1994) (see Johnson 1996). Copyright cases are continuing, assisted by the website called the House of Aboriginality. It should be noted that even when cases are determined in favour of the plaintiff, often the terms of settlement are not fulfilled due to the difficulty of imposing determinations.

[4] To demonstrate the widespread incorporation or Aboriginal imagery in Australian design, a group of indigenous artists built the House of Aboriginality, a mock house full of indigenous-derived objects (Johnson 1996).

[5] For example, there was heated public debate when the ex-partner of the winner of the 1996 Telstra National Aboriginal and Torres Strait Art Award, Kathleen Petyarre, argued that he should share in the award as he had helped paint the winning work.

[6] The 2001 acquisition by the National Gallery of Australia of the painting, 'All that big country from the top' by Rover Thomas for a record $800.000 raised a storm and a belief that the value of Aboriginal art had gone through the roof. The furore was quelled when similar figures were not obtained in 2005 for works of similar provenance by major auction houses (Maslen 2005). Between 2001 and 2006, the top selling Aboriginal artworks sold for between Aus$212,000 and AUS$778,000 (Australia Council 2006 Attachment 1). Nonetheless, the episode signalled a major shift in the way in which Aboriginal art was treated in the curatorial world and marketplace.

[7] These include Tracey Moffatt, Lin Onus, Kathleen and Gloria Petyarre, Rosella Namok, Judy Watson, Rover Thomas, Ginger Riley, Gordon Bennett, Richard Bell, Queenie McKenzie, Dorothy Napangardi, and the Tjapaltjarri's (Billy Stockman, Clifford Possum and Mick Namarari).

[8] This case study draws on an earlier publication (Craik, McAllister and Davis 2003).

Chapter 6: Managing creativity and cultivating culture

Let us briefly summarise the case developed in this monograph.

Government ideas about how to support arts and culture were traditionally very limited in their success and effectiveness. Historically, governments spent little on culture and what was spent tended to be earmarked for the elite arts sector. Arguably this support was not motivated by ambitions to broaden awareness of culture more generally in the community, but by notions of 'showcasing' endorsed representations of elite culture. Support was given to major signature institutions which constituted an oasis of culture, often situated in major cities.

Gradually, a greater range of activities began to be classified as 'culture' and from the 1960s onwards, governments were persuaded to invest more widely in these various cultural activities. Two things happened in parallel: government financial support widened to include many new and different forms of culture (films, festivals, events, more institutions, local community developments), and the older forms of arts patronage became more and more expensive to operate and sustain (owing to escalating costs, increased investments, artistic purchases, artistic salaries, and bureaucratic administration). These parallel developments put considerable pressure on the system.

On the supply side, production expanded as more people were able to practice various artforms and the costs of participating became more manageable to intending contributors. Changing technologies, better equipment, new media and more variable inputs meant that the arts and cultural sector was now more accessible to potential contributors. The sector became wide open to new players, not due to the policies of the old elite guard but due to initiatives of the new participants themselves. Some of these developments were welcomed by the arts habitués. So, for example, there was a spectacular growth and interest in special interest arts — such as indigenous and multi-cultural 'folk arts'. Much of this was not necessarily 'traditional' artistic expression but was reinvented through the use of new styles and techniques against the backdrop of traditional cultures (as with Aboriginal dot paintings done in acrylic).

On the demand side, the old arts sector did not highly value the size or diversity of its audiences. The sector operated as a self-referential 'closed shop' that, in practice, only expected to engage with itself. Artists and the cognoscenti were the intended audience and often were the sole revolving audience for elite arts presentations. The sector was organised and ruled by ideas of excellence and elite peer taste. But again, pressures from the 1960s onwards posed challenges to the insular *status quo*. Governments wanted to widen the reach of the arts and adopted the twin mantras of access and equity. They wanted to stimulate greater mass demand and engagement with forms of cultural expression.

However, attempts to widen access and improve equity have met with only limited success. The high arts sector has not necessarily approved of the government's aim to make the arts more accessible. It is not unknown for arts bureaucrats to give 'lip service' to all forms of culture in their 'impact' reports to government (such as CD sales, attendance at popular music events, gardening, and folk festivals) only to subsequently ignore these sectors once the case has been made about 'accessibility' or the funding request has been submitted.

Meanwhile, 'new' or non-traditional entrants in the sector compete for the marginal funds remaining after the elite organisations and institutions have secured their 'cut'. The result is often unsatisfactory for many players. In responding to claims of 'crisis' and 'reduced funding' (usually on an organisational basis rather than across the cultural field as a whole), governments face a dilemma. Should they pick cultural winners and reinstate forms of patronage or should they institute new funding models and force organisations to compete and meet new regimes of accountability and performance criteria?

Supporting elite arts that are demonstrably not self-sustaining attracts criticisms of *elite nurturing* while the application of competitive regimes is condemned as inappropriate *economic rationalism*. To avoid either charge, numerous governments have adopted a compromised or 'instrumentalist' approach that uses art and culture to leverage broader social outcomes in other more demonstrably 'needy' or 'deserving' portfolios (such as art programs in hospitals, prisons or for the mentally ill; cultural training schemes for unemployed or 'at risk' youth; art and cultural projects for marginalised or disadvantaged groups). Yet, this approach, too, has proved problematic.

Today's Challenges

The major challenges facing governments with respect to supporting the arts and cultural sector are:

- to what degree should governments be locked into supporting arts and culture;
- how best to address the imbalance between the sustainability of different sub-sectors of arts and culture;
- choosing appropriate policy models to achieve measurable outcomes; and
- demonstrating the effectiveness of whole-of-government approaches to arts and cultural policy.

These challenges are outlined in brief below.

The Drip-feed of Government Support

Contemporary governments seem to be inevitably and inextricably committed to supporting arts and culture. Given that, what options do they have and what are the consequences of adopting certain strategies over others? Generally, three basic models of support have been employed by governments:

- *patronage strategies* through which cultural activities are underwritten through direct public funding;
- *indirect funding* through diverse models of delivery including arms' length agencies such as art councils, ministerial directorates and departmental arrangements; and
- *facilitative strategies* designed to build philanthropic, sponsorship and partnership liaisons between culture and public and private sector agencies, clients and communities.

Concurrently, a bureaucratic culture of arts administration has burgeoned, bringing with it myriad managerial-style interventions in funding and evaluation.

Governments have struggled to justify the adoption of 'mix-and-match' approaches to arts and culture. Among the justifications frequently offered are:

- *boosterism*, involving the sustained promotion or 'talking up' of strategies;
- *instrumentalism*, through which 'culture' is used to leverage solutions for social, economic and cultural disadvantage;
- *cultural capital*, in which arts and culture curricula in public education are used to build 'cultural competence';
- *branding and recognition*, using culture to enhance international competitiveness, brand awareness and export potential;
- *citizenship*, by embedding culture within notions of citizenship and national identity; and
- *cultural or creative industries*, in which culture is viewed an 'industry' capable of demonstrating commercial viability and success within the constraints of broader consumer culture (cf. Jowell 2004, 2006; cf. Holden 2004, 2006).

The result is that governments at all levels now support more forms of culture than ever before and for more diverse reasons. Although there is talk of budget cuts or shortfalls, total government spending on the arts and culture is increasing. Governments are funding this sector, both *directly* (in the form of agencies and programs) and *indirectly* via strategies such as tax expenditures. Culture is certainly on the agenda but at what cost?

In many cultural forms, such as the performing and visual arts, arbitrary attempts to change support mechanisms have in fact compromised their potential for sustainability and created what may amount to a permanent dependency on support. Meeting enhanced accountability requirements often results in an increased cost burden that is not compensated by increased box office takings, merchandising or franchising revenue. In short, if these artforms are forced to undertake more activities in order to fulfil accountability requirements, they risk becoming less economically viable and sustainable (MPAB 2004).

Some level of government subsidisation of the arts and cultural sector appears to be inevitable. Government support for the arts is a double-edged sword, as the accountability requirement attending funding provision is often perceived as a source of 'interference' with the creative nature of the endeavour. This is especially so with the elite forms of culture that are under increasing pressure from a combination of rising costs, declining and aging audiences and other competing forms of culture. Governments, therefore, find themselves unable to resist calls to support both elite and marginal cultural forms. Furthermore, they are susceptible to the arguments of insider lobbyists and elite institutions (as Australia's cycle of reviews including the *Nugent Report* demonstrated).

We need to ask why governments accede to special pleading by elite arts and, furthermore, why established elite arts are unable to stand on their own two feet? Furthermore, does a resort to direct subsidy or co-funding undermine efforts to shift the funding burden to the private sector and community partnerships?

Sustainable versus Non-sustainable Arts and Cultural Sub-sectors

The second challenge facing governments is dealing with the uneven profile of the arts and cultural sector. The tradition of supporting expensive and generally non-sustainable artforms has largely persisted and settled into 'patronage plus' models. Arguments about market failure as the rationale for providing support for services and activities that are perceived as 'public goods' are not sufficient to explain why there is always support for elite and less popular arts and culture irrespective of party ideology or the type of support model that underpins the policy. Indeed, support flows even when there is no clearly articulated policy by government. In such circumstances, 'policy' tends to rely on 'back of envelope' largesse strategies, or 'accidental policy'. There are no market or economic rationalist arguments that can succinctly or persuasively be cited to justify continued support for traditional elite culture.

Yet support for this sub-sector continues to be at the heart of cultural policy even when placed within a broader cultural planning framework (such as Richard Florida's creative classes or Robert McNulty's sustainable communities approaches, see McNulty 1986; Ciccarelli and Coppa 2001). In fact, if anything, we are witnessing a re-emergence and reinforcement of bifurcation in the domain of arts and culture with a retreat to earlier forms of patronage for the top of the arts hierarchy and the propulsion of broader notions of culture into a *compote* of policies brought together under the umbrella of well-being, sustainability, entrepreneurship, citizenship and innovation.

As discussed earlier, the broad cultural arena or *eco-culture* that links to the everyday and popular cultural forms consumed by the majority of the population is of marginal interest to cultural policy makers despite its self-evident resonance with the community. Furthermore, one of the ironies of the instrumentalist approach to cultural policy is that it simultaneously ghettoises elite culture *and* alienates potential new audiences, resulting in perverse policy outcomes reminiscent of Jowell's *spiral of decline*. So while new cultural forms such as physical circus and indigenous art continue to prosper, older forms such as classical performing arts and mainstream visual arts still struggle.

Evaluating the Effectiveness of Policy Models

The third challenge for arts and cultural policy internationally is the difficulty of justifying and measuring whether different policy options actually work. In every advanced country there is some ongoing debate about the effectiveness of diverse models or suites of cultural support. Typically, one country's lament over its inadequate policy model is another country's ideal or proposed solution. America envies levels of funding in Europe. Countries with arms' length arts council envy American patronage. Direct funded countries envy both. The UK's lottery approach has generated plenty of investment and activity but has not necessarily guided the direction of that cultural explosion. And so it goes.

Attempts to measure the outcomes and effectiveness of arts and cultural policy — even where an explicit and limited instrumentalist strategy is employed — seem doomed to failure. Various commentators suggest that the purported outcomes of investment in the arts cannot readily be translated into measurable indicators, apart from the most basic statistics (audience size, ticket or product sales or practitioner income). Reliable measures of cultural capital or enhanced citizenship remain hard nuts to crack. Further, many evaluations are conducted at the end of a project with no or little attempt to conduct longitudinal or comparative studies of the impact of a program on artistic taste or cultural participation.

A complicating factor is that the policy choices in this domain seem to be intimately tied with broader policy, political and ideological dispositions — not to mention cultural history — in ways that cannot simply be addressed by adopting another funding model. In this sense, arts and cultural policies seem to be more locked into the nuances of the past than other policy arenas. This seems to restrict contemporary policy options more so than in some other portfolios where radical changes in governmental objectives and global trends has resulted in significant re-structuring, for example, the fashion (clothing, textile and footwear) industry.

Against this backdrop, governments appear less able to re-invent their policy models to fit new circumstances and so existing policy pathways and approaches are repeated. It would require a major re-think of policy processes to abandon traditional forms of arts and cultural support and engineer genuinely new approaches. In particular, the arms' length arts council model — so fêted in the past — seems particularly resistant. Although the failure of such approaches to achieve desired ends has been demonstrated, there is little indication of a mood to supplant these models with more effective policy machinery.

Criticisms of arm's length agencies are commonplace and have included such things as peer review bias (for or against particular applicants and artforms); a monopolistic or closed shop mentality that excludes anything new or different; misuse of financial and administrative arrangements; niche 'cognoscenti' bureaucratisation of arts and culture against trends in public administration in other agencies; and insufficient funds to broadly underwrite cultural activity in the public interest. In a number of jurisdictions, arts councils have had their ambit and breadth cut back by a variety of competitors in the cultural policy fields, be that government departments, ministerial largesse, community or private sector partners other levels of government.

Moreover, policies often have had unintended consequences that have undermined the ability of central cultural policy agencies to deliver effective policy outcomes. It is tempting to argue that the elite arts council model of cultural policy is outdated and counter-productive for efficient and effective arts and cultural policy. But are the alternatives — ministerial portfolio, administrative bureaucratisation, philanthropy, partnerships, cultural democracy — any better policy options? The question remains: should these monopolistic arts agencies have to compete with alternative cultural organisations for policies, strategies, funding largesse and clients?

Should Arts and Cultural Policy be a Niche Portfolio or a Broad Governmental Responsibility?

The fourth and final challenge to arts and cultural policy identified in this monograph is whether arts and culture requires a specialist policy approach or whether it should underpin government policy as a whole. In recent years, there has been a trend towards *whole-of-government* (or 'joined up') approaches to cultural policy as part of the broader definition of culture and its scope in everyday life. Yet the question needs to be asked as to whether this has undermined the integrity of cultural policy as a distinctive domain of public policy.

The answer appears to be yes and no. In some ways, the whole-of-government approach has been counter-productive and reactionary. In the area of traditional and elite arts there has been a return to forms of traditional patronage models or what might be called *neo-patronage* (old wine in new bottles). But in other arenas, there has been a proliferation of forms of art and culture outside the sanctioned domain of government agencies and largesse. Examples include physical theatre, digital media, multi-media, cross-platform visual and performing arts, indigenous art and performing arts, 'ethnic' and community artforms, 'street' and youth arts, and so on. These forms of culture resist patronage and often occupy spaces outside sanctioned cultural domains. They tend to be cost-effective, sustainable and even profitable as well as merging (or making irrelevant) the distinction between creator, audience and consumer.

These new forms of arts and culture perhaps pose the greatest challenge to existing policy rationales and options. The combination of changing public perceptions, trends in cultural participation and recent patterns of investment, support and partnership in art and culture have created a demand for models of cultural support that are based on community and creator-generated strategies of cultural enervation and exploration. Critics of such new policy approaches, however, warn of the limits to a policy framework driven by cultural democracy and popularity (e.g. Lammy 2006). Nonetheless, fractures within the conventional cultural policy community, together with challenges from new players, make re-thinking the tenets of arts and cultural policy a priority.

Much contemporary cultural vitality and energy is occurring outside the traditional arts and culture political framework and increasingly challenges the philosophy underpinning it. Examples include circus (physical theatre), new media arts, youth arts, performance culture consumed outside official parameters (CDs, DVDs), sub-cultures, community groups, amateur artists and performers, and electronically networked/produced/consumed arts and culture. These diverse examples of arts and culture are informing the development of active citizenship and cultural competence on various levels — local, regional, national, sub-cultural and global.

In the face of this challenge from below, some arts organisations have acknowledged the need to step outside their comfort zones and redefine the ambit of 'the arts' in contemporary society and social change. As Jennifer Bott said, in her last speech as the CEO of the Australia Council:

> If the arts are to impact on all Australians, it needs to enter communities of interest — and draw government, media and corporate support. For that to happen, we need to put culture not at the end of the value chain, tacked on 'if and when' funds are available, but right at the start — and the heart — of community building and engagement, where it belongs. (Bott 2006)

But such rhetorical commitments run counter to real trends evident within the Australia Council. While its budget has doubled in a decade (from $72 million in 1996 to $152 million in 2006) largely in order to fund the major performing arts companies, its outreach capability has been compromised and engaged boards of community arts and new media have been cannibalised. As mentioned earlier, the appointment of former AbaF head Kathy Keele as CEO of the Australia Council signals a commitment to pursuing business models of support. It seems, once again, that little 'a' arts (popular cultural forms) is a useful rhetorical tool to trot out on occasions but culture still resides in the big 'A' end of privileged artforms (performing arts, visual arts, literature).

There is, however, abundant evidence that 'culture' is not the privileged domain of elite academies. Elite interests do not exercise a natural monopoly over arts and culture. In fact, arts and cultural practice (and consumption) thrive outside Culture's hallowed spaces: elite galleries and performing spaces. Broad-based culture is increasingly and insistently impinging on orthodox and elite sectors. Even so, traditional elite arts and culture remain privileged recipients of government support justified as the articulation of symbols of civility, cultural competence and international visibility. Yet, while audiences and consumers for elite artforms are declining, audiences for prosaic arts and culture are blossoming.

Perhaps, because of the pervasive reach of culture and media, participants in and consumers of everyday culture are confident about defending their choices and celebrating prosaic culture as the real backbone of community identity and sustainability. Yet, there is still a divide in policy terms between community cultural development and elite cultural subsidy.

When Raymond Williams (1976) defined 'culture' in his seminal book, *Keywords*, he noted that its earliest use was in the horticultural context of animal and plant husbandry or 'cultivation' (caring or tending). While later uses went on to emphasise self-improvement and intellectual, artistic or spiritual development, our present cultural trends suggest that contemporary culture has embraced earlier notions of cultivation amid a wide spectrum of competing definitions (Bennett, Grossberg and Morris 2005).

But there is still a divide between those arts linked to self-improving civilisation and those linked to survival civilisation. Most commentators continue to make a distinction between the latter (e.g. folk art, mass art and various natural traditions) and the former transnational institutions of art that connects the artistic practices of urban centres around the world (Carroll 2007:142). Governments, too, reproduce the divide in their contradictory mix of policies.

It seems that, if governments want to avoid endlessly retreating to patronage forms of support, then it is imperative that they re-think the basis of arts and cultural policy and develop coherent strategies for further development. This is the challenge if we are to revitalise government responsibility for, and commitments to coherent arts and cultural policies, thereby allowing culture's 'garden' to flourish.

Bibliography

Aboriginal and Torres Strait Islander Commission and Office of Tourism. 1997. *National Aboriginal and Torres Strait Islander Tourism Industry Strategy*. Canberra: ATSIC.

Aboriginal and Torres Strait Islander Commission. 1994. *Draft National Aboriginal and Torres Strait Islander Cultural Industry Strategy*. Canberra: ATSIC.

Aboriginal and Torres Strait Islander Commission. 1995. *ATSIC Cultural Policy Framework*. Canberra: ATSIC.

Adair, Anthony. 1999. 'Reforming Public Funding of the Performing Arts', *Policy* Winter, pp. 20-24.

Altman, Jon and Taylor, Luke. (eds). 1990. *Marketing Aboriginal Art in the 1990s*. Canberra: Aboriginal Studies Press.

Arts Hub. 2006. 'Indigenous Art Inquiry Launched', *Arts Hub Australia* 16 August (http://www.artshuub.com.au/ahau1/news/news.asp?Id=99546&ref).

Arts Queensland. 2006. *Queensland Arts Industry Sector Development Planning*. Brisbane: Queensland Government.

Arts Victoria. 2003. *Creative Capacity. Arts for all Victorians*. Melbourne: Arts Victoria.

Auditor-General of Australia. 1974. 'Australia Council for the Arts', Section 3, *Report of the Auditor General of the Commonwealth of Australia for the Year Ended 1974*. Canberra: AGPS.

Australia Council. 1983. *The Artist in Australia Today*. Sydney: Australia Council.

Australia Council. 1984. *What Price Culture?* Sydney: Australia Council.

Australia Council. 2000. *Australians and the Arts. A Report to the Australia Council from Saatchi & Saatchi Australia. Overview*. Sydney: Australia Council.

Australia Council. 2003. *Arts Facts*. Sydney: Australia Council.

Australia Council. 2005a. 'Australia Council Changes For the Future', Media release, 7 April (http://www.ozco.gov.au).

Australia Council. 2005b. 'Summary of Changes at the Australia Council', News, 7 April (http://www.ozco.gov.au).

Australia Council. 2006. Submission to the Senate Inquiry into Australia's Indigenous Visual Arts Sector's Terms of Reference. Submission No. 38). Sydney: Australia Council.

Australian Broadcasting Corporation. 2007. 'Forum Debates Future of Arts Funding'. (Reporter: Anne Maria Nicholson), *Lateline* (April 18) Sydney: ABC Television (transcript) (http://www.abc.net.au/lateline/content/2007/s1900941.htm).

Australian Bureau of Statistics. 2004a. 'Attendance at Museums', *Arts and Culture in Australia: A Statistical Overview, 2004* (reissue), Catalogue No. 4172.0, Canberra: ABS.

Australian Bureau of Statistics. 2004b. 'Attendance at Selected Cultural Venues and Events', *Arts and Culture in Australia: A Statistical Overview, 2004* (reissue), Catalogue No. 4172.0, Canberra: ABS.

Australian Bureau of Statistics. 2004c. 'Purchase of Arts and Crafts', *Arts and Culture in Australia: A Statistical Overview, 2004* (reissue), Catalogue No. 4172.0, Canberra: ABS.

Australian Gallery Directors Council. 1981. *Aboriginal Australia*. Sydney: AGDC.

BAM Special Edition. 2003. 'Story Place. Indigenous Art of Cape York and the Rainforest', *The Courier-Mail* 26 July, pp. 1-5.

Bardon, Geoff. 1979. *Aboriginal Art of the Western Desert*. Adelaide: Rigby Limited.

Bardon, Geoffrey and Bardon, James. 2004. *Papunya. A Place Made After the Story. The Beginnings of the Western Desert Painting Movement*. Melbourne: The Miegunyah Press.

Battersby, Jean. 1980. *Cultural Policy in* Australia. Paris: UNESCO.

Battersby, Jean. 2005. 'Innovation in the Arts', The Alfred Deakin Innovation Lectures, 7 May, Melbourne.

Baume, Michael Senator. 1993. *A Vision for the Arts in Australia*. The Coalition Arts Policy. Canberra: Office of the Opposition Arts spokesman Senator Michael Baume.

Baxter, Virginia and Gallasch, Keith. 2002. 'Size Matter: The Small-to-Medium Sector Issue' (www.realtimearts.net).

Belfiore, Eleonora and Bennett, Oliver. 2006. 'Rethinking the Social Impacts of the Arts', Paper to the Fourth International Conference on Cultural Policy Research, Vienna.

Belfiore, Eleonora. 2004. 'Auditing Culture. The Subsidised Cultural Sector in the New Public Management', *The International Journal of Cultural Policy* 10(2), pp. 183-202.

Bennett, Tony, Emmison, Mike and Frow, John. 1999. *Accounting for Tastes. Australian Everyday Cultures*. Cambridge: Cambridge University Press.

Bennett, Tony, Grossberg, Laurence and Morris, Meaghan. (eds). 2005. *New Keywords*. Oxford: Blackwell Publishing.

Bennett, Tony, Trotter, Robin and McAlear, Donna. 1996. *Museums and Citizenship: A Resource Book* (Memoirs of the Queensland Museum 39(1)), Brisbane: Queensland Museum.

Bennett, Tony. 1995. *The Birth of the Museum. History, Theory, Politics* London and New York: Routledge.

Borghino, Jose. 1999. 'For Art's Sake', La Trobe University Essay, *Australian Book Review*, November.

Bott, Jennifer. 2006. 'The Australia Council: A CEO's Reflections', Speech to the Pacific Edge Regional Arts Australia National Conference, Mackay, 15 September.

Bourdieu, Pierre. 1984. *Distinction*. London: Routledge.

Boyle, Stephen. 2006. 'Cultural and Economic Policy Objectives: A Case of Either/Or or Both?', Paper to the Fourth International Conference on Cultural Policy Research, Vienna.

Brown, Suzanne. 2003. 'Up to Those Old Tricks' (AbaF Awards 2003 Supplement), *The Australian* 8 August, p. 5.

Carey, John. 2005. *What Good are the Arts?* London: Faber & Faber.

Carrol, Noël. 2007. 'Art and Globalisation: Then and Now'. *Journal of Art and Aesthetics*. 65(1): 131-143.

Caruna, Wally. 1987. *Aboriginal Art*. London: Thames & Hudson.

Casey, Dawn. 1999. 'The National Museum of the 21st Century: The National Museum of Australia', Opening Address to National Museums: Negotiating Histories Conference, 12-14 July, The Australian National University, Canberra.

Caust, Jo. 2003. 'Putting the 'Art' Back into Arts Policy Making: How Arts Policy Has Been 'Captured' by the Economists and the Marketers', *International Journal of Cultural Policy* 9(1), pp. 51-63.

Caust, Jo. 2006. 'Censorship or Coercion: Government and the Arts in Difficult Times', Paper to the Fourth International Conference on Cultural Policy Research, Vienna.

Ciccarelli, Maura and Coppa, Susan. 2001. *Culture Builds Communities: The Power of the Arts to Strengthen Neighbourhoods* Washington: Partners for Liveable Communities.

Cirque du Soleil. 2007. 'Cirque du Soleil at a Glance', *Pressroom*, Cirque du Soleil Official Website (http://www.cirquedusoleil.com/CirqueDuSoleil/en/Pressroom/cirquedusoleil/factsheets/cds.glance.htm).

Clarke, Donovan. 1967. 'Robinson, Michael Massey (1744-1826)', *Australian Dictionary of Biography* Vol. 2, Melbourne: Melbourne University Press, pp. 387-389.

Cochrane, Susan. 2001. *Aboriginal Art Collections. Highlights From Australia's Public Museums and Galleries*. Sydney: Fine Art Publishing.

Comunian, Roberta. 2006. 'Sponsorship and Cultural Patronage: In Search of a Theoretical Framework', Paper to the Fourth International Conference on Cultural Policy Research, Vienna.

Cosic, Miriam. 2006a. 'Tenacious Cultural Renovator', *The Australian* November 18. (http://www.theaustralian.news.com.au/story/0,20867,20775004-28737,00.html)

Cosic, Miriam. 2006b. 'Towards an Inclusive National Narrative', *The Australian* 8 September, p. 16.

Cosic, Miriam. 2007. 'Uproar at Louvre's Cultural Diplomacy', *The Australian* January 9 (http://www.museumnews.net/DLink.asp?ID=152794)

Council for Aboriginal Reconciliation. 1994. *Valuing Cultures: Recognising Indigenous Cultures as a Valued Part of Australian Heritage*. Canberra: AGPS.

Craik, Jennifer, Davis, Glyn and Sunderland, Naomi. 2000. 'Cultural Policy and National Identity', in G. Davis and M. Keating (eds) *The Future of Governance*, Melbourne: Macmillan, pp. 158-181.

Craik, Jennifer, McAllister, Libby and Davis, Glyn. 2003. 'Paradoxes and Contradictions in Government Approaches to Contemporary Cultural Policy', *International Journal of Cultural Policy* 9(1), pp. 17-33.

Craik, Jennifer. 1996. 'The Potential and Limits of Cultural Policy Strategies', *Culture and Policy* 7(1), pp. 177-204.

Craik, Jennifer. 2005. 'Dilemmas in Policy Support for the Arts and Cultural Sector', *Australian Journal of Public Administration* 64(4), pp. 6-19.

Craik, Jennifer. 2006. 'Neo-Patronage Versus Feral Culture: Choices and Challenges in Cultural Policy', Paper to the Fourth International Conference on Cultural Policy Research, Vienna.

Cultural Ministers Council Statistical Working Group. 2001. *Cultural Funding in Australia Three Tiers of Government 1999-2000*. Canberra: National Centre for Culture and Recreation Statistics, Australian Bureau of Statistics.

Cultural Ministers Council Statistical Working Group. 2002. *Cultural Funding in Australia Three Tiers of Government 2000-2001*. Canberra: National Centre for Culture and Recreation Statistics, Australian Bureau of Statistics.

Cultural Ministers Council Statistical Working Group. 2003. *Cultural Funding in Australia Three Tiers of Government 2001-2002*. Canberra: National Centre for Culture and Recreation Statistics, Australian Bureau of Statistics.

Cultural Ministers Council Statistical Working Group. 2004. *Cultural Funding in Australia Three Tiers of Government 2002-2003*. Canberra: National Centre for Culture and Recreation Statistics, Australian Bureau of Statistics.

Cultural Ministers Council Statistical Working Group. 2005. *Cultural Funding in Australia Three Tiers of Government 2003-2004*. Canberra: National Centre for Culture and Recreation Statistics, Australian Bureau of Statistics.

Cultural Ministers Council. 2002. *The Report to Ministers on an Examination of the Small to Medium Performing Arts Sector*. Canberra: DCITA.

Cummings, Milton and Katz, Richard. (eds). 1987. *The Patron State. Government and the Arts in Europe, North America and Japan*. New York and Oxford: Oxford University Press.

Cunningham, Stuart. 2006. *What Price a Creative Economy?* Platform Papers No. 9, Sydney: Currency Press.

Department for Culture, Media and Sport. 2004. *Government and the Value of Culture*. London: DCMS.

Department of Communications and the Arts. 1994 *Creative Nation: Commonwealth Cultural Policy*. Canberra: AGPS.

DiMaggio, Paul and Muhktar, T. 2002. 'Arts Participation as Cultural Capital in the United States, 1982-2002: Signs of Decline', *Poetics* 32, pp. 169-94.

DiMaggio, Paul. 1987. 'Classification in Art', *American Sociological Review* 52, pp. 440-55.

Dimasi, Rita and Paech, Vanessa. 2004. 'The Australia Council's New Groove?' *Arts Hub Australia* 13 December (http://www.artshub.com.au).

Dow, Stephen. 2007. 'Canberra push on indigenous art carpetbaggers', *The Age* 22 June 2007. (http://www.theage.com.au/news/arts/canberra-push-on-indigenous-art-carpetbaggers/2007/06/21/1182019278425.html) (accessed 25 June 2007).

Drinnan, Neil. 2001. 'High Wired', *The Courier-Mail* (BAM Section), 15 August, pp. 1, 4.

Dyson, Julie. 2002. 'Dance and the SMPA Report' (www.realtimeartsnet).

Editorial. 2006. 'Fine Art of Outrage', *The Australian* 10 February, p. 17.

Florida, Richard. 2002. *The Rise of the Creative Class*. New York: Basic Books.

Florida, Richard. 2005. *Flight of the Creative Class: The New Global Competition Talent*. New York: HarperCollins.

French, Alison. 2002. *Seeing the Centre. The Art of Albert Namatjira 1902-1959*. Canberra: National Gallery of Australia.

Gallasch, Keith. 2005. *Art in a Cold Climate. Rethinking the Australia Council* Platform Papers No. 6, Sydney: Currency Press.

Gardiner-Garden, John. 1994. *Arts Policy in Australia: A History of Commonwealth Involvement in the Arts* Canberra: Department of the Parliamentary Library, Background Paper No. 5.

Glow, Hilary and Johanson, Katya. 2006. 'Cultural Policy in Crisis: An Australian Case Study', Paper to the Fourth International Conference on Cultural Policy Research, Vienna.

Gray, Clive. 1992. *Comparing Public Policies: The Case of Cultural Policy in Western Europe*, Occasional Paper No. 4, Leicester: Leicester Business School, Leicester Polytechnic.

Gray, Clive. 2004. 'Joining-Up or Tagging On? The Arts, Cultural Planning and the View From Below', *Public Policy and Administration* 19(2), pp. 38-49.

Gray, Clive. 2006. 'Commodification and Instrumentality in Cultural Policy', Paper to the Fourth International Conference on Cultural Policy Research, Vienna.

Hall, Rodney. 2005. ' Give Wings to the Arts', *Artlink* 25(3), pp. 23-25.

Hamby, Louise. (ed.). 2005. *Twined Together: Kunmadj Njalehnjaleken*. Gunbalanya, N.T.: Injalak Arts and Crafts.

Hausmann, Andrea. 2006. 'The Tightrope Walk Between Financial Bottlenecks, Bundling and Conflicts of Interest: An Evaluation of Development Tendencies in the Relationship Between Cultural Institutions and Private Sponsorship in Germany', Paper to the Fourth International Conference on Cultural Policy Research, Vienna.

Hawkes, Jon. 2001. *The Fourth Pillar of Sustainability: Culture's Essential Role in Public Planning*. Melbourne: Common Ground Publishing.

Helmrich, Michele. 2003. 'Art Encouragement Led to Awakening of Culture', Obituary of Geoffrey Bardon 1940-2003, *The Courier-Mail* 9 May, p. 20.

Hesmondhalgh, David and Pratt, Andy. 2005. 'Cultural Industries and Cultural Policy', *International Journal of Cultural Policy* 11(1), pp. 1-13.

Hill Strategies. 2005a. *Who Buys Books in Canada? A Statistical Analysis Based on Household Spending Data*. Ottawa: Canada Council for the Arts.

Hill Strategies. 2005b. *Consumer Spending on Culture in Canada, the Provinces and 15 Metropolitan Areas in 2003*. Ottawa: Canada Council for the Arts.

Hill Strategies. 2005c. *Key Stats on the Arts in Canada, May 2005*. Research for the Arts. Ottawa: Canada Council for the Arts.

Hillman-Chartrand, Harry and McCaughey, Claire. 1989. 'The Arm's Length Principle and the Arts: An International Perspective — Past, Present and Future', in Milton Cummings and Mark Davidson Schuster (eds) *Who's to Pay? The International Search for Models of Support for the Arts*. New York: American Council for the Arts, pp. 43-77.

Hogg, Robert. 2002. 'Myth and Markets: Australian Culture and Economic Doctrine', *Journal of Australian Studies* 72, pp. 235-241, (http://find-articles.com/p/articles/mi_go1667/is_200201/ai_n6810728).

Holden, John. 2004. *Capturing Cultural Value. How Culture Has Become a Tool of Government Policy*. London: Demos.

Holden, John. 2006. *Cultural Value and the Crisis of Legitimacy. Why Culture Needs a Democratic Mandate*. London: Demos.

Hooper-Greenhill, Eileen. (ed.). 1995. *Museum, Media, Message*. London & New York: Routledge.

Horne, Donald. 1984. *The Great Museum*. London and Sydney: Pluto Press.

Horne, Donald and Travers, Mary. (eds). 2001. *Imaginative Country*. Sydney: New South Wales Centenary of Federation Committee.

House of Representatives Standing Committee on Expenditure. 1986. *Patronage, Power and the Muse: Inquiry into Commonwealth Assistance to the Arts*. Leo McLeay, Chair. Canberra: Parliament of the Commonwealth of Australia.

Hunjet, Paula. 2006. 'Arts Sponsorship of the Viennese Companies', Paper to the Fourth International Conference on Cultural Policy Research, Vienna.

Industries Assistance Commission. 1976. *Assistance to the Performing Arts*. Canberra: AGPS.

Isaacs, Jennifer. 1992. *Desert Crafts. Anangu Maruku Punu*. Moorebank, NSW and Auckland: Doubleday.

Janke, Terri and Quiggin, Robynne. 2006. *Indigenous Cultural and Intellectual Property: The Main Issues for the Indigenous Arts Industry in 2006*. Report to the Australia Council, Sydney: The Australia Council.

Johanson, Katya and Rentschler, Ruth. 2002. 'The New Arts Leader: The Australia Council and Cultural Policy Change', *The International Journal of Cultural Policy* 8(2): 167-180.

Johnson, Vivien. 1996. *Copyrites. Aboriginal Art in the Age of Reproductive Technologies*. Touring Exhibition 1996 Catalogue. Sydney: National Indigenous Arts Advocacy Association and Macquarie University.

Johnson, Vivien. 1999. 'The House of Aboriginality. Copyright and Cultural Integrity Issues in the Merchandising of Aboriginal Imagery', (www.mq.edu.au/hoa/index.htm).

Jowell, Tessa. 2004. *Government and the Value of Culture*. Essay by the Minister for Culture, United Kingdom, May.

Jowell, Tessa. 2006. *SoS Speech to the City. Minister for Culture's Speech at Bloomberg*, March 14, London.

Keane, Michael. 2004. 'Brave New World. Understanding China's Creative Vision', *International Journal of Cultural Policy*, 10(3), pp. 265-279.

Keating, Paul. 1993. *Distinctly Australian, The Future of Australia's Cultural Development*. Canberra: Office of the Prime Minister, Hon. Paul Keating.

Keele, Kathy. 2005. 'The Business of the Arts — Programs of Facilitation, Nurturing and Relationship Development with the Private Sector'. *Australian Journal of Public Administration*. (64)4: pp. 3-5.

Kemp, Rod. 2006. 'Inquiry into the Indigenous Visual Arts Sector'. Media release, 15 August. Canberra: Office of Senator the Hon. Rod Kemp, Minister for the Arts and Sport.

Kobayashi, Mari. 2006. 'Administrative Reform and the Impact of Privatisation on Publicly Funded Arts Facilities in Japan', Paper to the Fourth International Conference on Cultural Policy Research, Vienna.

Lammy, David. 2006. *Speech by Minister for Culture at the Launch of Demos' 'Cultural Value and the Crisis of Legitimacy' Publication*. 29 March, London.

Landry, Charles and Bianchini, Franco. 1995. *The Creative City*. London: Comedia.

Lee, Hye-Kyung. 2006. 'Conceptualising the Contemporary British Cultural Policy: Reflexive Modernity, De-differentiation and Holistic Government', Paper to the Fourth International Conference on Cultural Policy Research, Vienna.

Lee, Terence. 2004. 'Creative Shifts and Directions. Cultural Policy in Singapore', *International Journal of Cultural Policy* 10(3), pp. 281-299.

Letts, Richard. 2002. *A Report, a Quick Scan, an Empty Gesture? The Examination of the Small to Medium Performing Arts Sector*' (www.realtimearts.net).

Lindqvist, Katja. 2006. 'The Stranglehold of Public Principals on Art Organisations — Evidence from Sweden', Paper to the Fourth International Conference on Cultural Policy Research, Vienna.

Macdonnell, Justin. 1992. *Arts, Minister? Government Policy and the Arts.* Sydney: Currency Press.

Madden, Christopher and Bloom, Taryn. 2004. 'Creativity, Health and Arts Advocacy', *International Journal of Cultural Policy* 10(2), pp. 133-156.

Madden, Christopher, Sacco, Pier Luigi and Blessi, Giorgio Tavano. 2006. 'Cultural Ministry and/or Art Council: Which Instrument for an Effective Cultural Policy?', Paper to the Fourth International Conference on Cultural Policy Research, Vienna.

Madden, Christopher. 2004. 'Making Cross-Country Comparisons of Cultural Statistics: Problems and Solutions', Working Paper No. 2. Sydney: Australia Council for the Arts.

Major Performing Arts Board. 2004. *Securing the Future: An Assessment of Progress 1999-2003.* Sydney: Australia Council for the Arts.

Major Performing Arts Inquiry (Helen Nugent, chair). 1999a. *Securing the Future. Major Performing Arts. Discussion Paper* Sydney: Australia Council.

Major Performing Arts Inquiry (Helen Nugent, chair). 1999b. *Securing the Future. Major Performing Arts. Final Report* Sydney: Australia Council.

Mandel, Birgit. 2006. 'Arts and Culture for Everyone? Attitudes Towards Culture and their Impact on Cultural Participation', Paper to the Fourth International Conference on Cultural Policy Research, Vienna.

Marr, David. 2005. *A Wallet Full of Censorship.* Phillip Parsons Memorial Lecture, Sydney.

Maslen, Geoff. 2005. "Big Rain' Ends in Drought', *The Age* 1 September.

Matarasso, Franco. 1997. *Use or Ornament? The Social Impact of Participation in the Arts.* London: Comedia.

Maynard, Margaret. 1995. *Fashioned From Penury. Dress as Cultural Practice in Colonial Australia.* St. Lucia: University of Queensland Press.

McCallum, John. 2002. 'Mailman Reprises Growing Up Black. Review of the 7 Stages of Grieving', *The Australian* 30 August, p. 14.

McCarthy, Greg. 2004. 'Postmodern Discontent and the National Museum of Australia', *Borderlands e-journal* 3(3) (http://www.adelaide.edu.au/vol3no3_2004/mccarthy).

McCarthy, Kevin, Ondaatje, Elizabeth, Zakaras, Laura and Brooks, Arthur. 2004. *Gifts of the Muse. Reframing the Debate about the Benefits of the Arts* Santa Monica: RAND Corporation.

McCaughey, Claire. 2005. *Comparisons of Arts Funding in Selected Countries: Preliminary Findings*. Ottawa: Canada Council for the Arts.

McCulloch-Uehlin, Susan. 2002. 'Desert Blooms', *The Weekend Australian Review* 12-13 October, pp. R14-15.

McDonald, Janet. 1998. "Brought to You By ...", *The Weekend Australian Review* R22-23 August, pp. 16-18.

McGuigan, Jim. 2005. 'Neo-Liberalism, Culture and Policy', *International Journal of Cultural Policy* 11(3), pp. 229-241.

McNulty, Robert 1986. *Return of the Liveable City*. Washington: Partners for Liveable Communities.

McSkimming Roy and Francine d'Entremont. 2005. *Legacy, Transition, Succession. Supporting the Past and Future of Canada's Arts Organisations*. Ottawa: Canada Council for the Arts.

Mendelsohn, Joanna. 2005. 'Philanthropy, Sponsorship, or Dinner?', *Artlink* 25(3), pp. 30-33.

Merli, Paola. 2002. 'Evaluating the Social Impact of Participation in Arts Activities', *International Journal of Cultural Policy* 8(1), pp. 107-118.

Mills, Deborah and Brown, Paul. 2004. *Art and Wellbeing*. Sydney: Australia Council for the Arts.

Mills, Deborah. 2007. 'The Necessity of Art.' *Dialogue* 26(1), pp. 33-42.

Moore, Mark. 2002. 'Managerial Imagination', in *Creating Public Value. Strategic Management in Government*. Cambridge, Mass. and London: Harvard University Press, pp. 13-23.

Mulligan, Martin. 2007. 'A Role for the Arts in Creating Community.' *Dialogue* 26(1), pp. 23-32.

Mundine, Djon. 2005. 'White Face, Blak Mask', *Artlink* 25(3): 17-19, 22.

National Centre for Culture and Recreation Statistics. 2005. *Cultural Funding in Australia. Three Tiers of Government 2003-04*. Canberra: Australian Bureau of Statistics.

National Museum of Australia Review of Exhibitions and Public Programs (John Carroll, chair) 2003, Canberra: DCITA.

National Museum of Australia. 2006. *Cook's Pacific Encounters. The Cook-Forster Collection of the Georg-August University of Göttingen*. Canberra: National Museum of Australia.

Neale, Margo. 1998. *Emily Kame Kngwarreye. Alkalkere. Paintings from Utopia*. Brisbane: Queensland Art Gallery and Macmillan.

Neale, Sue. 2002. 'Burning Bright', *The Australian Review Magazine* July, pp. 12-18.

O'Faircheallaigh, Ciaran, Wanna, John and Weller, Pat. 1999. 'The Arts Industry: Reluctant Clients', in *Public Sector Management in Australia*. (2nd ed.) Melbourne: Macmillan, pp. 273-289.

Obuljen, Nina. 2006. *Why We Need European Cultural Policies. The Impact of EU Enlargement on Cultural Policies in Transition Countries*. Amsterdam: European Cultural Foundation.

Parsons, Phillip. 1987 *Shooting the Pianist: The Role of Government in the Arts* Sydney: Currency Press.

Perkin, Corrie. 2006. 'No Friend of the Big Ego', *The Australian* 2-3 September, p. 19.

Perkin, Corrie. 2007a. 'Culture no longer has us reaching for our wallets'. *The Australian*. June 18, p. 16.

Perkin, Corrie. 2007b. 'Face of a Funding Body', *The Australian* February 22, p. 44.

Perkin, Corrie. 2007c. 'Private Passions'. *The Weekend Australian (Review)*. June 9-10, pp. 4-5.

Peterson, Richard and Kern, Roger. 1996. 'Changing Highbrow Taste: From Snob to Omnivore' *American Sociological Review* 61(5), pp. 900-907.

Pick, John. 1986. *Managing the Arts? The British Experience*. London: Rhinegold.

Pick, John. 1988. *The Arts in a State. A Study of Government Arts Policies from Ancient Greece to the Present* Bristol: Bristol Classical Press.

Pratt, Andy. 2005. 'Cultural Industries and Public Policy', *International Journal of Cultural Policy* 11(1), pp. 31-44.

Queensland Art Gallery Foundation. 2003. 'Indigenous Australian Art Appeal', brochure, Brisbane: QAGF.

Queensland Art Gallery. 1982. *Queensland Art Gallery. Selected Works*. Brisbane: Queensland Art Gallery.

Queensland Art Gallery. 2003. *Story Place. Indigenous Art of Cape York and the Rainforest*. Brisbane: Queensland Art Gallery.

Radbourne, Jennifer and Fraser, Margaret. 1996. *Arts Management. A Practical Guide*. Sydney: Allen & Unwin.

Radbourne, Jennifer. 1993. 'Models of Arts Funding in Australia', *AESTHETEx. Australian Journal of Arts Management* 5(1), pp. 44-57.

Report of the Committee of Enquiry into the Crafts in Australia. 1975a. *The Crafts in Australia. Volume 1. Report* (Kym Bonython, chair). Canberra: AGPS.

Report of the Committee of Enquiry into the Crafts in Australia. 1975b. *The Crafts in Australia. Volume 2. Appendixes* (Kym Bonython, chair). Canberra: AGPS.

Report of the Committee of Inquiry on Museums and National Collections. 1975. *Museums in Australia* (P. H. Pigott, chair). Canberra; AGPS.

Report of the Contemporary Visual Arts and Crafts Inquiry (Rupert Myer, chair). 2002. Canberra: DCITA.

Review of Australia's Symphony and Pit Orchestras (James Strong, chair). 2005. *A New Era — Orchestras Review Report* Canberra: DCITA.

Review of the Australian Film Industry (David Gonski, chair) 1997. Canberra: DCITA.

Review of the National Museum of Australia. Its Exhibitions and Public Programs (John Carroll, chair). 2003. A Report to the Council of the National Museum of Australia. Canberra: DCITA.

Rothwell, Nicholas. 2006. 'Scams in the Desert', *The Weekend Australian Inquirer* 4-5 March, pp. 19, 22.

Rothwell, Nicholas. 2007. 'Colour Fades into Shadow'. *The Australian*. June 22, p. 16.

Rowse, Tim. 1985. *Arguing the Arts. The Funding of the Arts in Australia*. Ringwood: Penguin.

Ryan, Judith. 2006. 'Of Paint and Possession', *The Australian* 7 February, p. 10.

Savage, Mike, Gayo-Cal, Modesto, Warde, Alan and Tampubolon, Gindo. 2005. *Cultural Capital in the UK: A Preliminary Report Using Correspondence Analysis* Working Paper No. 4, CRESC Working Paper Series. Manchester: Centre for Research on Socio-Cultural Change, University of Manchester.

Schuster, Mark. 2002. 'Sub-National Cultural Policy — Where the Action is: Mapping State Cultural Policy in the United States', *International Journal of Cultural Policy* 8(2), pp. 181-196.

Segers, Katia. 2006. 'The Power to Concern Oneself with the Useless: Business Sponsorship of the Arts In Flanders', Paper to the Fourth International Conference on Cultural Policy Research, Vienna.

Senate Standing Committee on Environment, Communications, Information Technology and the Arts. 2006. 'Inquiry into Australia's Indigenous Visual Arts and Craft Sector', Terms of Reference, Canberra: The Senate, Parliament of Australia.

Senate Standing Committee on Environment, Communications, Information Technology and the Arts. 2007. Indigenous Art — Securing the Future; Australia's Indigenous visual arts and craft sector. The Senate, Parliament of Australia.

Sexton, Jennifer. 2006. 'Elites Coloured View of Hart Works', *The Weekend Australian* 1-2 April, p. 10.

Sintas, Jordi López and Álvarez, Ercilia Garcia. 2002. 'Omnivores Show up Again: The Segmentation of Cultural Consumers in Spanish Social Space', *European Sociological Review* 18(3), pp. 353-68.

Smee, Sebastian. 2006. 'Hung Out to Dry', *The Weekend Australian* 1-2 April, p. 21.

Stevenson, Deborah. 2000. *Art and Organisation*. St. Lucia: University of Queensland Press.

Strickland, Katrina. 1999. 'Top This!', *The Weekend Australian* 8-9 May, pp. 16-18.

Strickland, Katrina. 2004. 'Review-Based Cycle Winds Up', *The Australian* 27 December, p. 9.

Throsby, David. 2001 'Public Funding of the Arts in Australia – 1900 to 2000' *Year Book Australia, 2001* Canberra: Australian Bureau of Statistics.

Throsby, David. 2003. 'Does the Australian Government Have a Cultural Policy?', *Dialogue* (Academy of the Social Sciences) 22(2), pp. 54-60.

Throsby, David. 2006. *Does Australia Need a Cultural Policy?* Platform Papers No. 7, Sydney: Currency Press.

Tuggeranong Arts Centre. 2007. *skin to skin: Miri KutjaraTjungu (souvenir catalogue)*. Canberra, Tuggeranong Arts Centre.

UNESCO-ANU Seminar on Public Support for the Performing Arts. 1969a. *Volume 1: Proceedings*. Canberra: ANU.

UNESCO-ANU Seminar on Public Support for the Performing Arts. 1969b. *Volume 2: Background Papers*. Canberra: ANU.

Van Oost, Olga. 2006. 'After the Modern Art Museum?', Paper to the Fourth International Conference on Cultural Policy Research, Vienna.

van Rees, K., Vermunt, J. K. and Verboord, M. 1999. 'Cultural Classifications under Discussion: Latent Class Analysis of Highbrow and Lowbrow Reading', *Poetics* 26, pp. 349-65.

Vestheim, Geir. 2006. 'Cultural Policy and Democracy: A Theoretical Approach'. Paper to the Fourth International Conference on Cultural Policy Research, Vienna.

Volkerling, Michael. 2000. 'Death or Transfiguration: The Future for Cultural Policy in New Zealand', *International Journal of Cultural Policy* 6(1), pp. 7-28.

Volkerling, Michael. 2001. 'From Cool Britannia to Hot Nation', *International Journal of Cultural Policy* 7(4), 437-455.

Walker, Kim. 2005. 'Different Parts, But Singing the Same Song', *The Australian* 18 November, p. 16.

West, Celine and Smith, Charlotte. 2005. "We are not a Government Poodle': Museums and Social Inclusion Under New Labour', *International Journal of Cultural Policy* 11(3), pp. 275-288.

Whitwell, Gregory. nd. 'What is Economic Rationalism?' Money, Markets and the Economy, Program 11 Transcript, ABS Radio (http://www.abc.net.au/money/currency/features/feat11.htm)

Williams, Raymond. 1976. *Keywords*. London: Fontana.

Withers, Glenn. 1982. 'Principles of Government Support for the Arts', in S. Goldberg and F. Smith (eds) *Australian Cultural History. Culture and the State in Australia*. Canberra: Australian Academy of the Humanities and the History of Ideas Unit, Australian National University, pp. 53-58.

Zalfen, Sarah. 2006. 'The Crisis of Culture and the Culture of Crisis — The Case of Opera', Paper to the Fourth International Conference on Cultural Policy Research, Vienna.

Appendix A. Typology of artforms by characteristics of sector

TYPOLOGY OF ART/CULTURAL FORMS BY INDUSTRY CHARACTERISTICS (LOW, MEDIUM, HIGH)				
ARTFORM	Dependence on government support	Economic potential	Audience size and Socio-economic profile	Diversity of sub-sectors
Opera	High	Low	Low / High	Low
Classical Ballet	High	Low	Low / High	High
Visual Arts (museums and galleries)	High	Low	Low / High	High
Symphony Orchestras	High	Low	Low / High	Low
Classical Music — Other	High	Low	Medium / High	Low
Broadline Drama	High	Low	Low / High	Medium
Niche Drama	High	Low	Low / High	High
Libraries	High	Low	Mixed / Mixed	Low
Festivals	Medium	High	Mixed / Mixed	High
Opera Spectaculars	Medium	High	Mixed / High	High
Musicals	Medium	High	High / Mixed	Medium
Dance Spectaculars	Medium	High	Mixed / Medium	High
Film	Medium	Medium	Mixed / Mixed	High
Crafts	Medium	Medium	Medium / Mixed	High
Contemporary Dance	Medium	Medium	Medium / High	High
Community Art / Development	Medium	Low	Low / Medium	High
Circus / Physical Theatre	Low	High	High / Mixed	High
Creative Writing (Children)	Low	High	High / Medium	High
CD	Low	High	Mixed / Mixed	High
Popular Music (bands, CDs, training)	Low	High	High / Mixed	High
Digital Arts / New Media	Low	Medium	Medium / Mixed	High
Fêtes and Fairs	Low	Medium	Mixed / Mixed	High
Creative Writing (Adult)	Low	Low	Low / Medium	High
Poetry	Low	Low	Low / High	High

Appendix B. Key moments in Australian arts and cultural policy development

This appendix contains a detailed historical periodisation of Australian arts and cultural policy (Chart B.1) and a chronology of major events in the sector arranged according to government regimes and major reports to government (Chart B.2).

David Throsby (2001) has identified three periods in Australian arts and cultural policy:

- 1900-1967, when an explicit policy was 'virtually non-existent';
- 1968-1990, when there was a 'rapid expansion' of arts and cultural organisations and policies; and
- 1990-2000, when there was a moderate expansion of the sector combined with the articulation of a broad cultural policy framework. This period also saw the development of an interest in the production of cultural statistics and monitoring of cultural trends in the light of policy shifts.

This seems to borrow from Jennifer Radbourne's model that also identifies three broad periods:

- 1940s-1967, establishment of Australian cultural organisations;
- 1968-1975, establishment of semi-government finding organisations; and
- 1975-present, arts as industry (Radbourne 1993).

By contrast, I would offer this more elaborate model of cultural policy development:

Chart B.1

Period	Characteristics
Pre-1900 -Federation **Establishment of Settler Cultures**	Colonial/state based models of cultural survival, moral regulation and assertion of settler independence.
1900-1939 **State Cultural Entrpreneurialism**	Early state cultural entrepreneurialism particularly through the establishment of the Australian Broadcasting Commission (e.g. orchestras, concert broadcasts, tours by overseas artists) and development of commercial cultural entrepreneurs (such as J. C. Williamson).
1940-1954 **Setting Parameters of Australian Culture**	Wartime state regulation of culture and communication; concern about external negative cultural influences (fascism, American black music, Hollywood films/popular culture) but apart from measures of regulation, 'all talk no action' in terms of cultural facilitation.
1955-1966 **Organisational Patronage**	During this period a number of cultural organisations were established with government playing the role of elite architect.
1967-1974 **Growth and Facilitation**	A period of growth and facilitation with a diversity of cultural organisations and funding bodies plus recognition of multiculturalism as an important influence on national cultural development.
1975-1990 **Access and Equity**	Continued policies of previous era with emphasis on the mantra of increasing access to cultural resources and addressing issues of equity and marginalisation.
1991-1996 **Cultural Policy and Cultural Industries**	Revision of the scope of cultural corporations and activities under new governance strategies and concepts of corporatisation and cultural industry models within Australia's first articulated federal cultural policy, *Creative Nation*.
1996-Present **The Review Cycle and Neo-Patronage**	Bifurcation of cultural policy between promotion of creative industries and sustainable cultural forms, and shoring up of unsustainable and elite cultural forms by a return to neo-patronage.

Major Events In Australian Cultural Policy

The following timeline draws together some major events in Australian cultural policy including governmentally-established inquiries, and sets this against incumbent government regimes, on the one hand, and major discourses or critiques of arts & cultural policy, on the other.

Chart B.2

Pre-1900- Federation Establishment of Settler Cultures	1818-19 Michael Massey Robinson, the colony's poet laureate was rewarded with the gift of two cows for his services. This is credited with being the first cultural grant in Australia.
	The late nineteenth century witnessed the establishment of state art galleries: 1861 National Gallery of Victoria; 1871 Sydney; 1880 Adelaide; 1895 Queensland; 1887 Hobart; and 1901 Perth.
1900-1939 State Cultural Entrepreneurialism	Barton Government (Protectionist Party) 1901-03
	1901 National Library established within the Parliamentary Library (independent building 1968)
	Deakin/Fisher (ALP) 1908-10
	1908-66 Commonwealth Literary Fund — the first explicitly cultural body/scheme funded by the federal government
	1912 Commonwealth Art Advisory Board
	1900-1930 160 silent films made
	Bruce Government (Nationalist) 1923-29
	1928 Royal Commission on Wireless (**Hammond** [4]: January 1927-October 1927/8 mths)
	1928 Royal Commission on the Moving Picture Industry in Australia (**Marks** [7]: May 1927-April 1928/11 mths)
	Lyons Government (United Australia) 1932-39:
	1935 National Film and Sound Archive established (statutory authority 1984)
	1938 Royal Commission on Performing Rights (**Owen** [1]: September 1932-May1933/8 months)
1940-1954 Setting Parameters of Australian Culture	Curtin Government (ALP) 1941-45
	1943 Arts Council of Australia (NSW division) followed by divisions in other states
	1944 National Archives (national cultural institution 1984)
	1945 National Film Board established
	Chifley Government (ALP) 1945-46
	1946 Sydney Symphony Orchestra; 1950 W.A. Symphony Orchestra; followed by same in all states
	Menzies Government (Coalition) 1949-66:
	1954 Royal Commission on Television (**Paton** [6]: February 1953-September 1954/18 months)
	1954 Australian Elizabethan Theatre Trust (EATT);
1955-1966 Organisational Patronage	1956 Elizabethan Trust Opera Company (became Australian Opera 1969);
	1958 National Institute of Dramatic Art established
	1962 Australian Ballet; plus Union Theatre Repertory Co (→ Melbourne Theatre Co) and Old Tote Theatre Co (→ Sydney Theatre Co)
	1964 Australia Council for the Arts (federal division)

1967-1974 **Growth and Facilitation**	Holt Government (Coalition) 1966-67: 1967 Harold Holt → Australia Council for the Arts (operational in 1968) followed by state govt. departments and statutory authorities 1967 Committee for Assistance to Australian Composers (Holt) Gorton Government (Coalition) 1968-71: 1969 Interim Committee for the Film and TV School (John Gorton) 1970 Australian Film Development Corporation (AFDC) → AFC 1975 McMahon Government (Coalition) 1971-72: 1972 Committee of Inquiry into the Crafts in Australia (**Bonython** 1972)[1] 1972 Australia Council for the Arts rationalised and separate board amalgamated into AC structure (7 boards), e.g. Commonwealth Literature Fund became Literature Board in 1973 Whitlam Government (ALP) 1972-75: 1972 ACA rationalised and separate board amalgamated into AC structure (7 boards), e.g. CLF became Literature Board in 1973 1973 Opening of Sydney Opera House 1973 Australian National Gallery's purchase of Jackson Pollock's *Blue Poles* causes outcry about wasted public money — Whitlam puts it on his Xmas card 1973 Australian Film and Television School established (1980 Australian Film Television and Radio School) 1974 Australian National Gallery formed (building opened 1982; later National Gallery of Australia) Expansion of symphony orchestras and state art galleries 1974 Committee of Inquiry into Museums and National Collections (**Piggott** 1974) 1974 Auditor-General 'Australia Council for the Arts', Section 3, report of the Auditor-General 1974, AGPS. 1975 Australian Film Commission established 1975 NAISDA (National indigenous dance training institution)
1975-1990 **Access and Equity**	Fraser Government (Coalition) 1975-83: (NB. The Whitlam govt. policies lasted thru the Fraser govt 1975-83) 1976 Industries Assistance Commission Inquiry into the Performing Arts: *Assistance to the Performing Arts* (Canberra: AGPS) 1977 Senate Standing Committee on Education and the Arts (1977). *Report on Employment of Musicians by the Australian Broadcasting Commission*. Canberra: The Acting Commonwealth Government Printer. 1978 10BA Tax concession scheme for film investment Hawke Government (ALP) 1983-91: Australia Council 1983 *The Artist in Australia Today* Australia Council 1984 *What Price Culture?* David Throsby and Devon Mills 1989 *When Are You Going to Get a Real Job?* (Sydney: Australia Council) 1984 Task Force on Education and the Arts for Young People (**Boomer** [11]: August 1983-November 1984/15 months) 1985 Cultural Ministers Council set up Statistical Advisory group who produced copious cultural statistics (under UNESCO guidelines) 1985 Cultural Ministers Council *Study into the Future Development of Orchestras in Australia: Report of the Study Group to the Cultural Ministers Council*. Canberra: APGS 1985 Tim Rowse *Arguing the Arts: The Funding of the Arts in Australia* (Ringwood: Penguin) 1986 **McLeay** *Patronage, Power and the Muse: Inquiry into Commonwealth Assistance to the Arts* (House of Representatives Standing Committee on Expenditure; Canberra: Parlt of the Comm. of Aust) 1987 Philip Parsons *Shooting the Pianist: The Role of Government in the Arts* (Sydney: Currency Press) 1987 Committee of Inquiry into Folklife in Australia (**Anderson** [3]: April 1986-August 1987/17 mths) 1988 Film Finance Corporation formed 1989 Review of Aboriginal Arts and Crafts Industry (**Altman** [3]: October 1988-March 1989/5 months)

1991-1996 **Cultural Policy and Cultural Industries**	Keating Government (ALP) 1991-96: Hans Guldberg 1991 *Cultural Funding in Australia: Federal, State and Local Government* (Sydney: Australia Council) 1992 Stuart Cunningham *Framing Culture* 1992 Justin Macdonnell *Arts Minister? Government Policy and the Arts* (Sydney: Currency Press) Waks, N. 1992 *Review of ABC Music Policy*. Unpublished Report 1993 National Portrait Gallery established (statutory authority 1998) David Throsby and Beverley Thompson 1994 *But What Do You Do for a Living?* (Sydney: Australia Council) 1994 *Creative Nation: Commonwealth Cultural Policy* (Canberra: AGPS) 1994 John Garden-Gardiner *Arts Policy in Australia: A History of Commonwealth Involvement in the Arts* (Canberra; Dept of the Parliamentary Library, Background Paper No. 5)
1996-Present **The Review Cycle And Neo-Patronage**	Howard Government (Coalition) 1996-Present: Cultural Ministers Council (1996a). *Structural Options for the Orchestral Network / Cultural Ministers Council Standing Committee Paper*. Unpublished Paper Cultural Ministers Council (1996b). *Cultural Ministers Council Meeting Minutes 17 December 1996*. Unpublished Paper 1997 Review of Australian Film Industry (**Gonski**: July 1996-February 1997/7 months) 1999 Major Performing Arts Inquiry *Securing the Future: Final Report* (**Nugent** [4]: December 1998-December 1999/12 months) (Canberra: Department of Communications, Information Technology and the Arts) 2000 Australian Business Arts Foundation (AbaF) established (formerly Australia Foundation for Culture and Humanities) 2001 National Museum of Australia opened 2002 Inquiry into the Contemporary Visual Arts and Craft Sector *Contemporary Visual Arts and Crafts* (**Myer** [1]: July 2001-May 2002/10 months) 2004 Major Performing Arts Board (2004). *Securing the Future: An Assessment of Progress, 1999-2003*. Australia Council for the Arts 2005 Review of Australia's Symphony and Pit Orchestras. *A New Era– Orchestras Review Report 2005* (**Strong** [3]: May 2004-March 2005/10 months) Department of Communications, Information Technology and the Arts 2005 *National Museum of Australia Review of Exhibitions and Public Programs* (**Carroll**): Jan 2003-July 2003/6 mths) National Museum of Australia 2006 *Inquiry into the Indigenous Visual Arts Sector* (Senate Standing Committee on the Environment, Communications, Information Technology and the Arts: 15 August 2006-June 2007?). The Senate, Parliament of Australia.

ENDNOTES

[1] Appointed by McMahon Government but terms of reference extended by Whitlam Government along with some membership changes.

Appendix C. Models of cultural policy

ROLE OF MODEL	WHERE USED	POLICY OBJECTIVE	FUNDING MECHANISM	STRENGTHS & WEAKNESSES
FACILITATOR	USA	Diversity	Tax expenditures and incentives	S: diversity of funding sources W: excellence not necessarily supported; valuation of tax costs; benefits for benefactors; calculation of tax cost
PATRON	UK, Australia	Excellence International standards	Arm's length Peer evaluation	S: support for excellence W: favours traditional elite artforms
ARCHITECT	France	Social welfare Industry assistance	Department and Ministry of Culture	S: relief from box office dependence; secures training and career structure W: Creative directives lead to stagnation and resistance
ENGINEER	Former Soviet countries, Cuba, Korea	Political education, National culture	Government ownership of artistic production	S: focus creative energy to attain political goals W: subservience; underground; counter-intuitive outcomes
ELITE NURTURER[1]	Major Organisational Fund (Australia)	Selective elite development	Direct government ongoing funding of cultural organisations	S: encourage excellence, financial stability W: insulates organisations from external influences/forces

Source: Adapted from Harry Hillman-Chartrand and Claire McCaughey (1989) 'The arm's length principle and the arts: an international perspective — past, present and future', in M. Cumming and M. Schuster (eds) *Who's to pay for the Arts? The International Search for Models of Support* New York: American Council for the Arts Books, pp. 54-55.

ENDNOTES

[1] NB. Cummings and Katz refer to this as the Elite Gambler model. I prefer the term Elite Nurturer since it involves cosseting chosen organisations rather than betting on them (see Craik 1996).

Appendix D. Definitions of cultural policy

Cultural policy refers to the range of cultural practices, products and forms of circulation and consumption that are organised and subject to domains of policy. Cultural policy studies examine how governments deal with cultural issues in terms of strategies of facilitation, regulation and shaping. (Craik 1995: 202)

There are two main definitions of the *scope* of cultural policy:

> **DEFINITION 1:**
>
> **Cultural Policy Refers to the Regulation of the Marketplace of Ideas and Creative Practice**
>
> This definition posits that cultural and creative activities occur in the community as part of everyday life. These practices, products and patterns of consumption become then object of government policy with the objective of shaping production and consumption, often in relation to the development of national culture or export potential.

- Cultural regulation may be intended or unintended.
- Forms of support may be direct or indirect.
- Patrons may be individuals (e.g. private philanthropists or aristocrats) or group (e.g. church, state, monarch or corporate sector).

> **DEFINITION 2:**
>
> **Cultural Policy Refers to Policies that Manage the Production, Distribution and Consumption/Use of Cultural Resources**
>
> This is a more hands-on definition that sees government as playing a lead role in directly managing the field of cultural production and creative activity. This may be through ownership of cultural bodies, direct employment of cultural practitioners, commissioning works and acting of impresario for touring.

- Culture refers to artistic and intellectual forms of life.
- Cultural policies aim to change the relationships between forms of cultural expression and ways of life.
- Policies work through governmental agencies that set the framework for the manifestation of cultural resources.

Appendix E. The objectives of cultural policy

Traditionally, cultural policy has emanated from notions of 'public good' that claim that investment in culture enriches a society and fosters national identity and culture. Advocates argue that cultural policy has four objectives:

1. Protecting the public from harm (e.g. violence, sexually explicit material, racial vilification, pollution, extreme politics by regulatory strategies such as censorship, laws and/or licensing regimes).
2. Protecting the public from external pressures (such as cultural imperialism from Hollywood, multinational domination and global merchandising by measures to shore up local cultural production such as tariffs, investment and import restrictions).
3. Conserving and protecting cultural resources for the future (such as cultural heritage, cultural icons, material culture collections by establishing institutions and programs to preserve and conserve cultural heritage in museums, educational programs and community cultural development).
4. Fostering desirable attributes of citizenship (through citizen incentives e.g. rewards, funding of libraries, public broadcasting, national celebrations and cultural organisations and activities).

Appendix F. Government expenditure (Commonwealth, state and local) on the arts in Australia ($ million)

YEAR	1968-69	1973-74	1980-81	1982-83	1988-89	1991-92	1992-93	1993-94	1994-95
TOTAL	4.3	27.6	47.4	65.4	139.1	452.2	441.1	489.8	594.7

YEAR	1995-96	1996-97	1997-98	1998-99	1999-00	2000-01	2001-02	2002-03	2003-04
TOTAL	593.3	668.7	672.5	701.3	567.6*	614.3	730.9	666.8	716.4

Source: The figures for 1968-1999 are taken from Throsby (2001); after that, the figures come from the publications produced by the Cultural Ministers Council *Cultural Funding in Australia: Three Tiers of Government 1999-2000, 2001-02, 2002-03* and *2003-04*. Because of changes in how these figures are compiled they are not always comparable (especially between 1998-99 and 1999-2000). In 1968, 60% of funding came from the states and 40% from the Commonwealth but by 1988-89, the Commonwealth accounted for 51% of funding, the states 36% and local government 12%. From 1990, the Commonwealth share began to decline and a greater share assumed by state and local government.

Categories included in these figures are: Literature and Publishing/Print Media; Art Galleries; Visual Art and Craft (and Photography); Performing Arts; Performing Arts Venues; Film and Video; Multimedia; Community Arts/Community Cultural Activities.

Excluded are: Zoological and Botanic gardens; Libraries and Archives; Museums; Cultural Heritage; Radio and Television Boadcasting; Administration of Culture; Public Halls and Civic Centres; National Parks and Wildlife Service; and Other Culture — not elsewhere classified (n.e.c.).

Appendix G. Summary of major inquiries into and reviews of Australian arts and cultural sectors

Appendix G.1. Report of the Committee of Enquiry into the Crafts in Australia (Kym Bonython, chair). 1975. *The Crafts in Australia. Volume 1. Report*. Canberra: AGPS.

The Bonython report into the crafts in Australia was the first inquiry into this sector. It was announced by Coalition Prime Minister William McMahon in 1971 and continued under the Labor prime ministership of Gough Whitlam. The committee presented its report in 1975. During this period, craft practice in Australia had undergone significant growth and recognition including the establishment of a Crafts Board within the Australia Council for the Arts in 1973.

The aim of the enquiry was to:

- enquire into the present general state of the crafts in Australia as a professional activity;
- report on the organisation, distribution and development of the crafts in Australia; and
- report and make recommendations to achieve the above objectives.

As there was little information about craft activity, workers, training or marketing, the committee undertook extensive surveying, interviews and fieldwork to establish some baseline information about the contours of the sector. This work remains the most comprehensive study of crafts in Australia to date.

The key issue identified by the committee was:

> That there is almost no understanding on the part of the community as to what the crafts are or what their role should be. They have been regarded principally as hobbies in Australia rather than as professional pursuits with a significant part to play in the economy.

As a result, the report continued, there was a lack of training pathways; accreditation processes; disparagement by the artistic community; lack of supplies of quality materials; parsimonious attitudes by the buying public; and lack of interest by the design-related industries. In Aboriginal communities — even though crafts are recognised as part and parcel of indigenous culture — the committee observed that Aboriginal people 'have become alienated from their crafts' and require government assistance to redress this situation.

Accordingly, the committee made a comprehensive suite of recommendations having the specific object assisting the crafts 'to develop effectively in this country' by improving the provision of relevant services and conditions while removing impediments to growth and sustainability concerning. These embraced a wide range of matters including: training; professional standards; publicity; sales tax and customs duties; supplies; selling and exhibiting; craft centres; country needs; industry and industrial design; craft organisations; aboriginal crafts; migrant craft; and community and leisure.

Although this broad package was not implemented in full, it has provided the framework within which the craft sector in Australia has been transformed as acknowledged in the Myer report into the Visual Arts and Crafts sector in 2002.

Appendix G.2. Industries Assistance Commission. 1976. *Assistance to the Performing Arts.* Canberra: AGPS.

The IAC inquiry into 'whether assistance should be accorded the performing arts in Australia and if so what should be the nature and extent of such assistance' was commissioned by Labor Prime Minister Gough Whitlam in October 1974 and published in December 1976, by which time the Coalition government of Malcolm Fraser was in power. Reflecting on the saga that it became, Justin Macdonnell (1992: 142-3) argued that it is 'doubtful if any government investigation has ever been so misrepresented and misunderstood, or vilified'. Whitlam later commented that he was glad it landed on Fraser's desk and not his.

Although it has retrospectively been identified as part of Fraser's 'hard line' economic policy, in fact the enquiry occurred because of controversy, fanned during Whitlam's tenure, about the direction of arts policy and the increasing 'arrogance' of the Australia Council. Ironically, the Australia Council and commercial performing arts lobbyists, who hoped that the IAC would be able to increase subsidy to the sector, unintentionally initiated the enquiry. It was some time before they realised that the IAC agenda was very different from their own, or Whitlam's, or Fraser's, for that matter.

The enquiry has been commonly represented as recommending the withdrawal of subsidy to the elite performing arts and therefore as a collective 'philistine', unappreciative of Australian culture. In fact, the IAC had what might now be seen as a progressive stance on arts and culture, beginning from the question of what constituted the arts and culture and what public benefit flowed to the community. Explicitly, it adopted a broad anthropological definition of culture and rejected the intrinsic value and special pleading of the elite sector. Witnesses, while passionate about the arts, failed to convince the Commission of the community benefits of the arts or the ways in which elite culture contributed to the Australian community's 'way of life'. It took a broad-brush definition of the performing arts as 'the entire range and ... not [just] to the narrow but highly subsidised group of arts which many witnesses invested with a intangible and undefined 'cultural' value'.

The Commission dissected the assumption that the 'flagship philosophy' should be subsidised in order to produce 'excellence' that would somehow, intangibly, enrich the community at large and the related belief that this was 'settled national policy'. Rather, this was a discriminatory policy that disregarded community values and the ordinary culture of citizens. To redress this, the Commission argued that arts and cultural policy should be based on the three criteria of innovation, disseminating and education, to which end, funding to the elite companies should be maintained for three years then phased-out over five. Funding should be re-directed towards the new objectives that met community expectations. Where existing [elite] companies failed to replace support by other means and show relevance, they might face the prospect of closure. The report concluded that:

> It has not, however, been able to discern any rational reason why the community as a whole should not adopt a partisan attitude toward distributing assistance from which it could not reasonably expect to benefit.

When the draft report was released, it stunned everyone: Whitlam, Fraser and the arts community included. Prime Minister Fraser distanced himself from it, rejecting the 'harsh economic criteria' and 'user-pays principle' it had employed and confirming a commitment to continue to support 'individual art [and] also the major performing arts companies in Australia — the opera, ballet, and drama'. Despite widespread criticism of the report and a new round of submissions and responses, the final report was largely unchanged. The government quickly rejected its findings to phase out 'existing patterns of assistance to the performing arts'. Rather, it enunciated its policy as follows:

> The Government considers that the promotion of excellence in the arts is of primary importance and continuation of assistance to the presently subsidised companies is seen as being consistent with this objective.

While the IAC report was officially dead, its musings on the elitism of the performing arts and its community of interest — especially the elitist fortress mentality of the Australia Council — slowly percolated through subsequent debates about the arts and cultural sector. It is fair to conclude that the logic of the report slowly transformed the terms in which arts and culture was discussed and eventually the basic premises on which policy strategies were couched.

Appendix G.3. House of Representatives Standing Committee on Expenditure (Leo McLeay, chair). 1986. *Patronage, Power and the Muse: Inquiry into Commonwealth Assistance to the Arts.* Canberra: Parliament of the Commonwealth of Australia.

This report came after a period of energetic development of the arts and cultural sector and expansion of policies designed to facilitate cultural activity. It was also responding to the furore that ensued on the release of the Industries Assistance Commission report of a decade before that had adopted a stringent rational economic framework of analysis.

The McLeay report was an attempt to define (or redefine) the role of the Commonwealth 'in assisting the arts'. The committee took a broad view of the arts as one component of culture and saw the role of government as one of maximising the benefits of the arts to society as a whole. Specifically, it rejected 'the view that Commonwealth assistance is a right of the arts because of their merits' and that 'arts assistance is a specialised form of welfare for artists'.

The Committee accepted that 'the arts are not homogeneous' and that different artforms provide different public benefits, thus requiring different mechanisms of support. In particular, the Committee distinguished between 'heritage art' (survivors of past artistic activity), 'innovatory art' (new methods of expression or interpretation of culture) and 'new art' (the mass of contemporary art work which falls into the mainstream of cultural activity).

Accordingly, the Committee recommended that heritage and innovatory art required mechanisms 'to sustain adequate levels of conservation of art' while new art should be prioritised because of its 'public benefits'. A key phrase of the report was: 'Access and diversity should thus be principal objectives of assistance to new art'.

The key objective:

> Of government arts assistance [was] increasing cultural democracy. We define this not as wider access to the so-called high arts, but rather as access by the community to a diversity of cultural experiences from which individuals may choose for themselves the cultural activities of most benefit to themselves at any time.

To this end, the report recommended that:

- the Australia Council confine its activities to the subsidised arts in the form of the administration of grants while the broader arts and cultural agenda be facilitated by a federal department, namely the Department of Arts, Heritage and Environment;

- in order to retain the professionalism of the major performing arts companies, they were centralised under the Australia Council to administer grants and institute accountability processes;
- an overhaul of tax concessions that were deemed 'relatively unaccountable', 'inequitable, inefficiently targeted and open ended' was proposed by instituting a system of Ministerial approval;
- support for popular contemporary music was recommended; and
- addressing alternative models of support, the Committee recommended establishing the International Cultural Corporation of Australia, Artbank, and the Public Lending Right Scheme.

The McLeay report set the scene for arts and cultural policy for the next decade.

Appendix G.4. Department of Communications and the Arts. 1994 *Creative Nation: Commonwealth Cultural Policy*. Canberra: AGPS.

In 1992, the Commonwealth Government appointed a Cultural Policy Advisory Panel of eminent Australians from diverse walks of life to advise on the formulation of a Commonwealth cultural policy.[1] The panel wrote a preamble based on the belief that 'democracy is the key to cultural value' in a world undergoing major changes in technologies, values and ideologies shaping the expansion of 'homogenised international mass culture'. Australian culture was defined as the sum of mode of life, ethics, institutions, manners and routines that has 'flourished' into 'an exotic hybrid'. While this should be encouraged, cultural policy makers faced a dilemma between reconciling egalitarianism with artistic excellence.

The panel concluded that culture should be placed higher among the government's policy priorities, both as a separate portfolio and across all areas of government. It also recommended that a Charter of Cultural Rights be adopted to guarantee all Australians: the right to an education that encourages creativity; the right to access cultural heritage; the right to new artistic works; and the right to community participation in cultural life.

The *Creative Nation* document that followed this preamble was premised on the assertion that culture defines national identity and preserves Australian heritage. As the 'first national cultural policy', *Creative Nation* aimed to link everyday life with cultural enrichment and the pursuit of cultural excellence.

It recognised the complex, multicultural and urban society that Australia had become as well as acknowledging the contribution of Aboriginal and Torres Strait Islander culture to national identity. Several aims underpinned its recommendations:

- to shore up our cultural heritage in national institutions;

- to adapt new technologies for cultural preservation and dissemination;
- to create new avenues for artistic and intellectual growth and expression; and
- to support artists and writers.

The policy was also grounded in the belief that 'this cultural policy was also an economic one. Culture creates wealth.'

Creative Nation canvassed a wide range of measures to enhance the role of culture in Australian life. This included expanding the role of the Commonwealth in managing culture through: increased federal funding; enhanced roles for DCITA and the Australia Council; establishing a Major Organisations Board within the Australia Council to support elite performing arts organisations; and establishing new cultural support programs and incentives to develop private sector cultural sponsorship.

As well as enhancing the role of cultural agencies and organisations, *Creative Nation* also proposed a range of strategies to address issues in the film and media sector; provide development funding for multi-media centres; introduce a range of measures to protect creative copyright; expand cultural heritage provisions; offer incentives for cultural industry development; redress cultural education provision; introduce incentives for cultural investment and export; and expand cultural tourism in Australia.

Although only some of the recommendations were introduced before the Keating Labor Government lost office in 1996, *Creative Nation* set the terms of arts and cultural policy in the early years of the Howard coalition government and influenced international models for cultural policy, most notably, in the United Kingdom.

Appendix G.5. *Review of the Australian Film Industry* (David Gonski, chair) 1997. Canberra: DCITA.

The Gonski review of the Australian film industry aimed at addressing structural problems in the industry, in particular, the extent to which it is marginalised through competition with the mainstream Hollywood film industry, its reliance on government funding to get film projects off the ground and the perceived need to make films that reflect and are relevant to Australian culture.

Australia is home to one of the world's oldest film industries, dating from the 1890s and boasting one of the largest cinema-going audiences in the world (in per capita terms). Despite this, the Australian film industry had been in abeyance until the 1970s when Australian governments initiated various funding schemes to encourage film production, especially for films that promoted national culture. Government initiated film organisations have included state bodies (e.g. Film Victoria, New South Wales Film and Television Office, Pacific Film and Television

Commission, ScreenWest and the South Australia Film Corporation) as well as a number of federal bodies: the Australian Film Commission (AFC) (1975-present), Australian Film Institute (AFI) (1958-present), the Australian Film Finance Corporation (FFC)(1988-present), Film Australia, and the National Film and Sound Archive (1984-present).

During the 1980s, the federal government introduced the *10BA Scheme*, which was a generous tax concession incentive, designed to stimulate film investment in film production. Despite a flurry of films, the scheme did not translate into better box office receipts or quality films and, despite various adjustments to the scheme, it was eventually replaced by investment mechanisms administered by the FCC.

Due to continued debate about the viability of the industry, David Gonski was commissioned to inquire into the Australian film industry and delivered his report in 1997. He calculated that the industry contributed $1.2 billion annually to the Australian economy and employed over 20,000 people. Gonski's approach was to downplay the 'screen culture' approach of film as a building block of national identity and examine its business basis and export potential. The release of the report produced mixed reactions. Despite concern about cutting government funding, existing arrangements persisted. A new initiative flowing from the Gonski report involved the establishment of a framework for the formation of Film Licensed Investment Companies (FLICs), a measure that conferred special status on a few film production companies to invest in innovative projects, drawing on government and private funding.

These arrangements were strengthened in 2001 when then Minister for Communications, Information Technology and the Arts announced new measures for supporting the film industry. These included:

- a new production incentive in the form of a refundable tax offset;
- increased funding for the FCC;
- new funding for SBS Independent to commission multicultural drama and documentaries;
- extra funding for Film Australia to fund its community service obligations in the form of films in the national interest;
- increased funding for digital and broadband services, development and education; and
- incentives to attract off-shore productions in Australia.

These changes were perceived by the critics within the film industry as shoring up the larger and more commercial players while ignoring the needs of independent and experimental producers.

Appendix G.6. Major Performing Arts Inquiry (Helen Nugent, chair). 1999. *Securing the Future. Major Performing Arts. Final Report* Sydney: Australia Council.

The Nugent inquiry into 31 major performing arts organisations arose out of a perceived crisis in the sector due to the adverse impacts of globalisation, technological change and demographic shifts on their viability: in short, costs were spiralling while revenue was declining. The inquiry conducted a comprehensive dissection of the sector employing a business model as well as a review of the organisations' performance in terms of training, administration and repertoire.

The report argued that the major performing arts companies made 'an enormous artistic and financial contribution to Australian life' and that the implementation of these recommendations would 'stabilise' and 'reposition' the sector and thereby 'secure [its] artistic vitality, accessibility and financial viability'.

The underlying principles of the report were that:

> Australia should have a vibrant major performing arts sector that enriches Australian life and builds its image as an innovative and sophisticated nation; that Australia should cost-effectively deliver broad access to the major performing arts — recognising that the arts are for everyone; an that Australia should have a financially viable major performing arts sector that supports artistic vibrancy.

Equally, however, the report endorsed the view that government support should be 'transparent and should be based on an understanding of the responsibilities of all parties'.

The report's 95 recommendations were accepted by government and an extra $70 million was injected into the sector by federal and state governments, administered by DCITA and the MPAB of the Australia Council. The recommendations were designed to create a cohesive structure for the industry and included:

- Classifying companies into Global, Australian Flagship, Niche and Regional Flagship depending on the strategic role played by each.
- Introducing a five step funding model that reflects the cost of each artform, each company's strategic role and the commitment to geographic access.
- Ensuring a commitment to invest in new works, new productions and improved quality of performance to increase box office receipts and build a differentiated image of Australia.
- Strengthening private sector support.
- Engaging in collaborations, cooperation and co-productions between companies within artforms.
- Exploring a 'community of musicians' concept between orchestras.

- Strengthening marketing and development capacity.
- Introducing rolling triennial funding.
- Improving accountability and reporting practices.
- Adopting a reserves policy.
- Changing the financial dynamics of companies in each artform.

Despite the introduction of the majority of these changes, the overall wellbeing of the major performing arts companies has not markedly improved, as an Australia Council review by the Major Performing Arts Board concluded in 2004. Because of the perceived bias towards protecting the major artform companies, other sectors lobbied for similar reviews and funding increases. The *Nugent Report* became the first of the so-called 'Review Cycle' into arts sectors with inquiries into the small-to-medium performing arts sector, visual arts and crafts, symphony orchestras, new media and dance to follow.

Appendix G.7. Australia Council. 2000. *Australians and the Arts. A Report to the Australia Council from Saatchi & Saatchi Australia. Overview*. Sydney: Australia Council.

In 1998, the Australia Council commissioned a consultancy to establish the extent to which the general public valued 'the arts'. This was part of a broader strategy to map the characteristics of the Australian cultural environment in which they hoped the arts would flourish in the future. Saatchi and Saatchi (through Sandra Yates and Paul Costantoura) conducted the research.

The research found that some sectors of the public hold misconceptions about what constitutes 'the arts' as well as misconceptions within parts of the arts sector about who constitutes the Australian public. The report concludes that both misconceptions need to be addressed if art and culture are to become more important to Australian life.

The main findings can be summarised as follows:

- While the arts have become part of Australian society, the majority enjoy art and culture associated with everyday life as a form of entertainment and a forum for social opportunities with friends and family.
- Many Australians do not feel welcome to enjoy the arts due to a perceived sense of exclusion, a lack of access, lack of relevant information and education about the arts, and negative connotations about the social environment of the arts.
- There is a relatively high level of disinclination towards or disengagement from the arts arising from a belief that they are irrelevant to people's lives.
- The arts sector does not communicate well with the general public outside specific markets.
- Some within the arts sector have inaccurate perceptions of the 'average Australian'.

- There is a lack of organisational skills, communication mechanisms, commercial and community foci, and marketing-cum-branding expertise within the arts sector.
- The future of the arts will require securing new supporters and markets from those Australians who currently largely ignore the arts.
- Australians are split into thirds in estimating the personal and national value of the arts: a third placing a high value on the arts; a third a low or fairly low value; and the rest in-between.
- Those who value the arts highly are likely to be: female, with university education, living capital city centres, without children, older and in households with high incomes.
- Those who place a low value on the arts find them irrelevant to their lives and feel excluded from them, finding them elitist and inaccessible.
- Familiarity with and knowledge of the arts from childhood is positively related to positive attitudes and likelihood of artistic participation.
- Few could name more than three components of 'the arts' spontaneously (the big 'A' arts) and wanted to include a broader array of little 'a' arts (e.g. fashion design, graphic design, popular music, television shows, and children's art and drama).
- Australians possess a much broader idea of creativity than is encompassed by 'the arts'.

Appendix G.8. Cultural Ministers Council. 2002. *The Report to Ministers on an Examination of the Small to Medium Performing Arts Sector*. Canberra: DCITA.

As a result of the funding changes that followed from the *Nugent Report* on the major performing arts sector, the small to medium performing arts sector (SMPA) lobbied for similar consideration and attention to their circumstances. In 2000, the Cultural Ministers Council commissioned 'an examination of the factors influencing the artistic and financial position of small to medium sized performing arts organisations'.

The SMPA report complimented the sector on its 'great diversity, a focus on new creative endeavour, a slim administrative structure, a large volunteer workforce and a commitment to artistic production'. However, it noted that the financial situation of the sub-sectors was 'finely balanced' or 'in decline', 'raising questions about the sustainability of organisations in [the music and dance] sectors in both the short and long term'.

The report noted that although the SMPA sector was hoping for increased government funding to alleviate its precarious situation, the working party suggested, 'there are other solutions which also need to be considered'. The included:

- clarification of governments' expectations of the SMPA sector either towards greater self-sustainability or excellence in artistic development (by either supporting fewer organisations or targeted increases to specific organisations);
- strengthening the administrative capacity of the SMPA sector to provide a more stable business and operating environment (by training, board membership, resource networking across the sector, audience development, and fundraising);
- improved inter-governmental communications and co-funding arrangements; and
- enhancing the role of the SMPA sector in promoting Australia's culture in the international arena by facilitating international tours.

The report was published in 2002 but, unlike the *Nugent Report*, no new financial arrangements resulted. This led to widespread resentment within the SMPA sector who believed that, although it was the 'research and development' incubator for experimentation and innovation in Australian performing arts, the SMPA sector was languishing while the less efficient, larger and more conservative major organisations were receiving generous recurrent funding and enjoyed favourable financial arrangements with increased subsidy. Little has come from the SMPA report although it initiated the collection of data on the characteristics of the sector.

Appendix G.9. Report of the Contemporary Visual Arts and Crafts Inquiry (Rupert Myer, chair) 2002. Canberra: DCITA.

This report, another in the Review Cycle, was commissioned in 2001 by then Minister for the Arts and the Centenary of Federation, Peter McGauran, and chaired by Rupert Myer. It explored opportunities to 'to identify key issues impacting on the future sustainability, development and promotion' of the visual arts and crafts sector recognising that:

> Visual arts and crafts are major contributors to Australian culture and the Australian economy, yet at the same time, visual artists and crafts people are amongst the lowest income earners in Australia. This inquiry ... will give us a comprehensive picture of the sector and what can be done by all tiers of government to ensure its continued development in the future.

The report concluded that the sector required an injection of funding:

> ... for individual artists and their supporting infrastructure from corporate sponsorship and private philanthropy. This is not intended as a substitute for government support but as a critical supplement.

It was a broad ranging inquiry into the estimated 20,000 visual artists and craft practitioners as well as curators, arts writers, arts organisations and galleries.

Despite the enthusiasm and dynamism of the sector, the inquiry found that financial foundations were generally vulnerable even though the sector was estimated to contribute approximately $160 million to GDP. There was concern in the sector that its contribution was not 'sufficiently valued' and its achievements not 'adequately acknowledged'. A comprehensive analysis of the sector was compiled.

A wide range of recommendations were made, including:

- increased government funding across all tiers;
- implementation of a resale royalty scheme;
- revision of taxation liabilities of artists;
- revision of copyright provisions;
- protection of indigenous copyright and intellectual property rights;
- strengthen the role of arts and crafts organisations to provide supportive environment for artists;
- extend schemes for touring, exhibitions and audience development; and
- implement schemes to encourage sponsorship and philanthropy (such as tax incentives and a cultural gifts program).

In all, an extra $29 million was injected into the sector. While the spirit of the report was accepted and some recommendations adopted, more recent studies of artists' incomes and infrastructural support suggest that major reform of this sector has not occurred.

Appendix G.10. *Review of the National Museum of Australia. Its Exhibitions and Public Programs* (John Carroll, chair). 2003. A Report to the Council of the National Museum of Australia. Canberra: DCITA.

The National Museum of Australia opened in 2001 and immediately attracted controversy on a number of fronts including: the postmodernist choice of architecture (in the shape of a rainbow serpent); the small size of the building; the choice of exhibition themes and their interpretation; the use of facsimile objects for display; the *high tech* presentation of exhibits; and the perceived privileging of indigenous culture over that of European settler culture.

The government's stated intention in establishing the museum was:

> That the museum would be an institution, combining the best contemporary techniques with new media technologies, in order to offer a range of experiences of wide appeal. There were to be permanent, changing and travelling exhibitions and blockbusters, and it was intended that audiences beyond Canberra would be reached using information and communication technologies.

The Museum was charged with celebrating 'our journey as a nation' in social history spaces. Prime Minister, John Howard, took particular interest in the NMA and its Council was stacked with members sympathetic to the government's conservative outlook. Controversy continued, however, and in 2003, a review was announced into the exhibitions and public programs of the Museum. Specifically, the review, chaired by the widely respected sociologist, John Carroll, was to consider:

- whether the Museum had complied with its prescribed role and functions;
- whether the government's vision had been realised; and
- offer recommendations on future priorities.

In reality, the review was a politically-driven inquisition into the policy and operations of the Museum. One of the issues underpinning the review was the divide between those who advocated a chronologically, classificatory and authoritative view of Australian history and society versus those who advocated a 'pluralist' presentation of 'imagined communities', multiple histories and diverse points of view. A number of related themes emerged during the review, such as:

- What is the role of a national museum?
- How do contemporary museums differ from traditional ones?
- How can museums relate to different kinds of visitors (one-off, frequent, children, Australians, international visitors, etc.)? and
- How should objects be displayed and explained?

After a comprehensive review of the activities of the NMA and a vigorous public submission process, the committee concluded that the Museum would need to make some changes if it was to fulfil its potential as an authoritative cultural institution. It found that the NMA had met its founding criteria 'to varying degrees' however, the committee concluded that its 'principal weakness is its story-telling':

> The NMA is short on compelling narratives, engagingly presented dramatic realisations of important events and themes in the Australian story. And there are too few focal objects, radiant and numerous enough to generate memorable vignettes, or to be drawn out into fundamental moments ... Without engagement, there is little likelihood of inspiration, reflection or education.

Singled out for criticism was the *Horizons Gallery* that addressed post-European parts of the Australian story but failed to present 'exemplary individual, group and institutional achievements' central to understanding 'the fundamental themes and narratives of Australia'. The review also found 'difficulties with signage, exhibit lighting and acoustics — ones which are pervasive and serious'. Lack of coordination between research, collection policy and collaboration was also noted. The review identified a strengthening of the Museum's story-telling capacity and the use of focal objects as the core of a desired long-term strategy while making a number of short-term recommendations including:

- reconsidering the themes and narratives for the Horizons and Nation galleries;
- addressing curatorial issues and exhibition modes;
- redeveloping the introductory film, Circa to provide a 'compelling introduction to the Museum, and a clear orientation to the permanent exhibitions'; and
- conducting better research, collaborative and audience development activities.

Appendix G.11. Review of Australia's Symphony and Pit Orchestras (James Strong, chair). 2005. *A New Era – Orchestras Review Report* Canberra: DCITA.

The last of the so-called 'Review Cycle' inquiries examined the state of symphony and pit orchestras, arguably the least viable of the performing arts sector. Commissioned by then Minister for the Arts and Sport, Rod Kemp, in 2004, it was mooted during the MPAI to address 'clear financial pressures and other challenges' facing Australian orchestras.

Chaired by James Strong, the committee examined a range of operational, marketplace, financial and governance issues facing Australian orchestras focusing on artistic vibrancy, cost effective access, financial viability and financial transparency. 20 recommendations were made including:

- divesting the six symphony orchestras from the ABC and transform them into public companies limited by guarantee;
- changing the employment and superannuation provisions of orchestra employees;
- improving the expertise of boards and revising appointment practices;
- developing a new realistic funding model;
- removing the efficiency dividend;
- cutting the number of players in Queensland orchestras (from 85 to 74), Adelaide Symphony Orchestra (from 75 to 56) and Tasmania Symphony Orchestra (from 47 to 38); and
- inquiring into the provision of orchestral services for Opera Australia and the Australian Ballet.

The report triggered considerable heated public debate, attracting more attention than any of the other reviews. Especially contentious was the recommendation to reduce the size of certain orchestras, a change that was pilloried by cartoonists and commentators. This recommendation was quietly dropped. Generally, however, the Strong recommendations were accepted resulting in:

- an extra $25.4 million over four years;
- extra funding to retain orchestra sizes in Queensland, South Australia and Tasmania;
- funding to transform orchestras into public companies;
- funding for occupational health and safety changes;
- funding to offset the efficiency dividend; and
- extra funding for providing orchestral services to Opera Australia and the Australian Ballet.

Subsequent studies of the state of Australia symphony orchestras suggest that these changes have failed to achieve stability and financial well-being.

Appendix G.12. The Senate Standing Committee on Environment, Communications, Information Technology and the Arts. *Indigenous Art, Securing the Future: Australia's Indigenous visual arts and craft sector* (Senator Alan Eggleston, Chair) (June 2007). Canberra, The Senate.

In August 2006, the Senate established a Committee for inquiry into Australia's Indigenous visual arts and craft sector, with particular reference to:

- the current size and scale of Australia's Indigenous visual arts and craft sector;
- the economic, social and cultural benefits of the sector;
- the overall financial, cultural and artistic sustainability of the sector;
- the current and likely future priority infrastructure needs of the sector;
- opportunities for strategies and mechanisms that the sector could adopt to improve its practices, capacity and sustainability, including to deal with unscrupulous or unethical conduct;
- opportunities for existing government support programs for Indigenous visual arts and crafts to be more effectively targeted to improve the sector's capacity and future sustainability; and
- future opportunities for further growth of Australia's Indigenous visual arts and craft sector, including through further developing international markets.

The report, published in June 2007, made 29 key recommendations. Among its key recommendations were:

- That the Commonwealth establish a new infrastructure fund to assist Indigenous visual arts and craft; that this fund complement existing NACIS program funding; that this infrastructure fund be for a sum of the order of $25 million, made available over a period of five years; and that the fund be administered by DCITA.

- That the Commonwealth further expand funding under the existing NACIS scheme and consider revising its guidelines to confine its use to non-infrastructure projects.
- That, in light of the special circumstances facing Indigenous artists in the Alice Springs area, a proposal be developed, including a funding bid, for an art centre in Alice Springs that will cater for artists visiting the town from surrounding settlements.
- That, as a matter of priority, the ACCC be funded to increase its scrutiny of the Indigenous art industry, including conducting educational programs for consumers as well as investigation activities, with a goal of increasing successful prosecutions of illegal practices in the industry.
- That the Indigenous Art Commercial Code of Conduct be completed as soon as possible.
- That, once completed, all Commonwealth, state and territory agencies apply the Indigenous Art Commercial Code of Conduct where appropriate, including when purchasing Indigenous art.
- That, once completed, all stakeholders in the industry examine, disseminate and adopt where relevant the Indigenous Art Commercial Code of Conduct.
- That the industry be given the opportunity to self regulate. If after two years persistent problems remain, consideration should be given to moving to a prescribed code of conduct under the Trade Practices Act.
- That as a matter of priority the government introduce revised legislation on Indigenous communal moral rights.
- That the Commonwealth support increased efforts to showcase Indigenous visual arts and craft internationally.

At the time of writing, the report, having been only recently released, had not made a discernable impact.

ENDNOTES

[1] The panel consisted of: broadcaster Jill Kitson, cartoonist Bruce Petty, arts entrepreneur Leo Schofield, artist Michael Leslie, designer Jenny Kee, academic Peter Spearritt, author Rodney Hall, author Thea Astley, filmmaker Gillian Armstrong and dancer, Graeme Murphy.

www.ingramcontent.com/pod-product-compliance
Lightning Source LLC
Chambersburg PA
CBHW040548220526
45473CB00027B/3041